INFORMAL LECTURES ON
FORMAL SEMANTICS

SUNY Series in Linguistics
Mark Aronoff, Editor

INFORMAL LECTURES ON FORMAL SEMANTICS

Emmon Bach

State University of New York Press

Published by
State University of New York

© 1989 State University of New York

For information, address State University of New York
Press, State University Plaza, Albany, N.Y., 12246

Library of Congress Cataloging-in-Publication Data

Bach, Emmon W., 1929–
    Informal lectures on formal semantics.

    Based on lectures presented at a Summer Institute
of Linguistics at Tianjin Normal University in 1984.
    Bibliography: p.
    Includes index.
    1. Semantics. 2. Semantics (Philosophy) I. Title.
P325.B27   1989   415   87-26719
ISBN 0-88706-771-9
ISBN 0-88706-772-7 (pbk.)

10 9 8 7 6 5 4 3 2 1

CONTENTS

Words are not just blown air. They have a meaning. If you are not sure what you are talking about, are you saying anything, or are you saying nothing? Words seem different from the chirping of birds. Is there a difference or isn't there? How can Dao be so obscure and yet admit of truth and falsehood? How can words be so obscure and yet admit of right and wrong? How can Dao cease to exist? How can words not be heard?

Zhūang Zǐ

FOREWORD

In the summer of 1984, I was invited to take part in a Summer Institute of Linguistics at Tianjin Normal University and gave a series of six lectures on current issues in formal semantics. This book is based on those lectures. Although the number of chapters has been increased, I have retained the form and style of lectures in order to help keep my goals clearly in mind.

Formal semantics—better, model-theoretic semantics—for natural language is a field that has risen rapidly in the last decade and a half. I believe it is an exciting area of study which has produced a large body of interesting results and new questions. Yet, because of the rather formidable technical apparatus it commands, it has remained something of a closed book for many linguists and others interested in the phenomenon of natural language. In designing my Tianjin lectures, and in turning them into this book, I have been guided by three self-imposed constraints: first, I presuppose nothing at all in the way of previous work in formal semantics; second, I have tried to tell no lies; third, I have endeavored to keep strange formalism to the minimum. Within these constraints, my aim has been to provide a groundwork in model-theoretic semantics and a sampling of issues, results, and open questions that workers in formal semantics are currently concerned with.

Rather than beginning with a possibly daunting presentation of introductory matter, I have chosen to introduce technical material gradually as it is needed. The first three lectures amount to a rather condensed presentation of possible world semantics as it was used by Richard Montague. Subsequent lectures take up a number of topics of current interest. Naturally, I could not hope to survey all currently "live" topics. The choice of topics is obviously influenced by my own interests and the current research being conducted in my home environment at the University of Massachusetts in Amherst. I would like to thank those who have helped to make that environment what it is, both past and present, as well as the many friends and colleagues in other places from whom I have learned, above all my "relations-in-intention" here, Angelika Kratzer and Barbara H. Partee. I also acknowledge gratefully the help of Angelika Kratzer, Polly Jacobson, and two anonymous reviewers, who gave me many valuable comments on the manuscript. Special thanks to Kathy Adamczyk, who not only typed up the tapes from the actual lectures given in Tianjin but added immeasurably to their interest by her uproarious interpolations and additions, unfortunately not contained herein, and to Molly Diesing for help with proof-reading and the index.

August 10, 1987
Amherst, Massachusetts

Lecture I:

BACKGROUND AND BEGINNING

Today's lecture has two parts. One of them is a very general introduction where I will talk about the question: "What is meaning?" and say a little bit about the history of semantics—the study of meaning—in recent and not so recent linguistics. And then we will begin, right away today, with a more specific introduction to a more technical subject, the study of semantics from a certain point of view, that of model-theoretic semantics. This is the general topic of the eight lectures.

Although what we understand about the semantics of natural language is surely very much less than what we do not understand, I believe some progress has been made in the last 15 years or so. I also believe that we are currently in the midst of a number of quite exciting developments, and I would like to concentrate here on some of these developments. I intend these lectures to be largely self-contained. I do this for two reasons. The first is that I would like the lectures to be accessible to everyone that is here, and I'm sure that you have a wide variety of backgrounds. More important, I believe strongly that it should be possible for a specialist or technician to explain what he or she is doing to anyone who is interested and who is willing to go along and do a little work, and that trying to do this is important for me also, because it forces me to think hard about why I am doing what I do and whether it is important. Specialists can get caught up in the details of their work and forget why it is that they do what they do.

I apologize that I am so ignorant of the linguistic tradition of your country. There are not very many places in the world where an independent linguistic tradition has developed; China is one of them. I spent the first years of my life in Japan, and enough of my early experience has remained with me to help me recognize that China has been to the East what Greece and Rome have been to the West. And wherever we have records of the earliest intellectual wonderings of humans, we find records of people wondering about language. Some of the questions people have asked are these:

Why are there so many different languages?
How different and how much alike are different languages?
What is the relation between language and the world?
How can words be so obscure and yet admit of wrong and right?

The last question is from Zhūang Zĭ in a passage from *The Inner Chapters*. The passage raises some very central questions that we will consider here. It also presents very clearly the central assumption of semantics. I quote: "Words are not just blown air, they have a meaning." The main job of semantic theories is to explain how words and other linguistic expressions, such as sentences and phrases, can have meanings and to say what these meanings are. I think that this point, that linguistic expressions have meanings, is very obvious, and that the ordinary person would consider it so obvious that he or she would suppose that linguists, those people whose job it is to understand language, would naturally take semantics, the study of meaning, to be one of their central concerns. Yet, this has not always been the case in the history of linguistics. I will say a little bit about this history today.

Now what could a meaning be? Again, I think the ordinary person would say that a meaning must be something that is not language, except in the case of words about words. Words refer to things. Sentences are about happenings in the world. We use words and sentences to talk about the world, about our own feelings and concerns and needs. Once again this point seems obvious, but linguists and philosophers who have concerned themselves with language have not always agreed. We will take up this question at several points in these lectures. The point of view that I will follow there is one that makes two assumptions:

I. Language has meaning.
II. Meanings are things that are not language.

What are meanings? Meanings are the things that language is about. This is apparently what makes words different from the twitterings of birds, which are not *about* anything, as far as we can tell. Semantics is the study of the meanings that expression of language can have.

So far, I've used the word *meaning* for something that linguistic expressions have and semantics is about. But this word itself—the word *meaning*—has many meanings as does the corresponding verb *mean*. Some of these different meanings can be illustrated in a few examples.

1. Giving you these flowers means that I love you.
2. Those mountains ahead mean trouble.
3. He said that he would join us, but he didn't mean it.
4. When I say X, I mean Y.
5. *Àiren* means *spouse*.

In working out a scientific theory, we have to be careful about the terms we use. We often have to adopt special terminology that departs from ordinary language and gets its meaning from the way in which it is used in our theories. Let us agree to continue to use *meaning* as a term to cover lots of different kinds of relationships, but we will adopt some special terminology for the more special and technical aspects of *meaning*.

In order to focus on some of these more specialized ideas that we need to use, let us consider the examples just given and what they seem to mean. In the sentence, "Giving you these flowers means that I love you," I do a certain act, I give you some flowers; by this act, I want to convey to you something about my feelings for you, that I love you. So *mean,* the English word *mean* in this sentence, seems to designate a relation between an act that I do and some meaning, intention, feeling, or attitude that the action is supposed to convey. This is not the sense of *meaning* that I want to focus on here.

Or consider the example: "Those mountains ahead mean trouble." This seems to mean something like this: "Continuing our journey (or whatever) is going to be hard for us because we will have to cross those mountains." So here, *mean* seems to designate a relation between something—the mountains—and some consequence for us with respect to some purpose or goal. This, again, is not the sense of meaning that I want to focus on here.

Consider the next examples: "He said that he would join us, but he didn't mean it." This seems to concern questions of sincerity. Someone says something, but does he really mean it? That is, is he really sincere in what he says? Here, *mean* seems to designate a relation between a person and something that that person says. Again, this is not the sense of *meaning* that I want to focus on here, although there will be some points where we will take up the kind of question raised by this example having to do with language and what people do with language.

The next example—"When I say X, I mean Y."—seems to mean something like this: I say something, there is a usual meaning associated with what I say, but I am telling you that what I really intend to convey to you is something different. So here *mean* has to do with the relation between a person, something that he says, and something else that he, the person, means by that. This example requires references to the kind of *meaning* I want to concentrate on here, but it still does not directly express that sense.

Let us now look at the last example: "*Airen* means *spouse.*" This example is closely related to the sense of *meaning* I want to start with here. What are we talking about? You will notice that I have underlined the Chinese word *airen* and the English word *spouse*. A more precise way of stating what this example is intended to mean is: The word *airen* means the same thing as what is meant by *spouse*. What I want to focus on here is, what is it that we mean by "the same thing?" *Airen* means this thing and *spouse* means this thing. What is the thing that these two words mean or designate? Let us call this thing, whatever it is, the *denotation* of the linguistic expression in question. So, another way of saying the same thing is to say, the denotation of this word, *airen,* is the same as the denotation of *spouse*. And again we are talking about something that is not a feeling but something in the world, whatever it is that is referred to by these two words. Now this is still not quite right. The trouble is that without reference to a language, we do not really know what these quoted expressions are supposed to be. There might be a different language in which something like this word *airen* meant a certain kind of flower and another language in which *spouse* meant newspaper or something like that. So, to be very definite about it, we need to say something like this: The denotation of *airen* in a certain language (Chinese) is the same as the denotation of *spouse* in English. Therefore, when we talk about denotations of expressions, we presuppose that we know that there is a certain language that the expression is being used in.

Now, I have just given a very quick look at what I take semantics to be, or at least some important part of semantics. Let us reflect on what will be required for such a view of semantics to work. Evidently, this program has two parts. First, we need to show how to assign denotations to all the basic or lexical elements in the language, Chinese, English, or whatever. And then, we need to show how to put together the denotations of the simple expressions, words like *spouse* or *airen,* and to show how the denotations of complex expressions can be made from the denotations of the simple ones. And so on, and so on, and so on.

Here is a simple example of what we need to do. Suppose we say that *John* denotes a certain individual—me, for instance, or any particular person whose name is John. And suppose that we say that *walk* denotes a certain set or collection of individuals—the set of walkers. To be able to say what "John walks" means, we want to say something like this: it is a true statement to say that the individual denoted by *John* is a member of the set of individuals that walk. That is a very simple example of how we might want to treat the meaning of complex expressions by putting together the meanings or denotations of the expressions that go into them, as we make more and more complex expressions in our syntax.

So, we apparently need two kinds of things, thus far, to talk about the denotations of expressions in a language. We need to be able to talk about individuals, to have a set of individuals that are denoted by words like names. John is one such individual. And we need to be able to talk about sets or collections of the individuals. Consequently, in giving this example of what a denotation might be as part of an answer to the question, "What is meaning?" I have already made a certain choice. The choice is that denotations are something like things in the world, not language but things in the world—people, tables, cups, books, and so on. That is the main kind of theory I will be talking about here. But it is important to know that other kinds of answers could be given and have been given. One such answer is that meanings are mental objects of some sort, things in my head, concepts or thoughts. So, the answer I have adopted is a controversial answer. Not everyone will agree with that choice.

I would like to put this question aside for now and for the next few lectures simply assume that an interesting way to talk about meanings is to talk in this way about the denotations as being things, sets of things, and so on. Later in the lectures I will return and look at some of the other sorts of answers that might be given to the question, "What is a meaning?" and compare different theories with different answers to the question.

Before we begin to look more closely at a semantic theory, I would like to spend a few minutes on the recent history of linguistic theory in the United States and Europe. The year 1957 was an important one in linguistics. That was the year in which Noam Chomsky published his small book *Syntactic Structures*. This book had a profound impact on linguistic theory, not only in the United States but in many other parts of the world. To my mind, the most important idea and the one that was hardest to grasp for linguists who had worked in earlier traditions was the idea of a generative grammar.

What is a *generative grammar?* It is supposed to be an explicit statement of what the classes of linguistic expressions in a language are and what kind of structures they have. This notion is important for us here because the kind of semantics that I wish to concentrate on presupposes the existence of an explicit grammar of this sort. Therefore, I want to spend a little time reflecting on what such a grammar is and what it does. The most important thing to keep in mind, and the one thing that is hardest to become accustomed to at first, is the idea that the grammar actually says explicitly what is in the language. That is the basic idea of a generative grammar. An example will make this idea more concrete. Given a generative grammar of a language, it should be possible for you to construct various kinds of expressions in the language by completely mechanical means, without knowing anything about the language ahead of time. So, I want to present a small grammar for a small artificial language that will be important for us as we progress. And I would like to develop it to illustrate what we are thinking about.

I will call this language *PC* (an abbreviation for predicate calculus). PC has several kinds of expressions. It has what I call *terms*, and they are of two sorts:

1. *variables,* and these will look like this:
   x, y, z, . . . (late letters of the English alphabet);
2. *individual constants,* and they are chosen from these letters
   a, b, c, . . . (early letters of the English alphabet); and
3. it has further expressions, two sorts of *predicates,* that we will call *one-place predicates,* and these will be expressions like *Run, Walk, Happy, Calm, ...*

(You may think that this is English, but it is not English. For our purposes right now, think of them as simply meaningless symbols that belong to these different classes of expressions.) And then we will have *two-place predicates.* And these will be words again that look like English, but are not:

Love, Kiss, Like, See, ...

These are the only kinds of basic expressions or, if you like, *lexical expressions* in the language. I included ellipses here because we may imagine many more of them exist, but we only need a few examples of each kind. The other expressions in our language have to be constructed by rules I now give you to show you how to make some more complex expressions. So, we are going to make one further class of expressions, which I will call *formulas.* Here are the rules for making formulas:

R1. If *P* is a one-place predicate and *T* is a term, then *P(T)* is a formula.

This means if I pick something that is a term, an *x* or *y* or *a* or *b* and pick something that is a one-place predicate, I can construct a formula by putting together the first thing—say *Run*—and writing the second thing—a term like *a*—in parentheses after it: so *Run(a)* would be a formula according to this first rule. You can probably guess what the second rule is:

R2. If *R* is a two-place predicate and *X* and *T* are terms, then *R(X,T)* is a formula.

So, we can now write things like this: *See(a,b).*

This is only the syntax of the language. There is no semantics for the language at this point. But given this grammar, we can already say about certain expressions that they belong to certain classes in the grammar because we have said explicitly what these classes are. So we know for example that the expression x is a term and that b is a term. And we know that these are formulas in the language:

Run(x), Like(c,y), Calm(c), and *Love(x,y).*

And, while we do not know anything about what they mean, we have, in effect, a very simple generative grammar for this language PC. All we need to generate examples from this language is to be able to recognize the symbols or signs and to check whether they belong to the appropriate categories or classes that are listed in the grammar.

The grammar that I have just given—for a very simple language—follows the form that logicians like Carnap and Tarski use to define the syntax of the formal languages of symbolic logic and other artificial systems. It is an example of what some people call a "formal system." One way of characterizing what Chomsky did is to say that Chomsky put forward a certain thesis or hypothesis about natural languages, namely, that a natural language, a language like Chinese or English, can be described as a formal system. And I call that "Chomsky's Thesis" from 1957. Chomsky's way of constructing a grammar was rather different from the way in which I presented this language. But a simple system like the one I have illustrated is enough for us to begin. In a later lecture, I return to the question of what kind of grammars seem most appropriate for natural languages like English or Chinese.

The PC language is not very interesting at this point because we can only make very simple sentences. We cannot make anything very complicated, and there are many things we cannot express in this language, so I want to add two further rules about formulas. The first new rule says:

R3. If F is a formula then so is this: $-F$.

the fourth rule says:

R4. If F and G are formulas so are these two things:
    (F & G) and *(F ∨ G).*

Theses rules tell us that we can make more complicated formulas out of simple ones. We can take one formula and another formula and put them together with a sign in between and parentheses around and we will have another new formula. We can take that formula and put the sign " $-$ " in front of it and we will have another formula. So, now we can make sentences that are as long as we want from this grammar.

Grammars for natural languages also must have this capacity because there is no longest sentence in any language. If you give me a very long sentence in English I can always add something to make it more complex and make a longer sentence out of it. With these rules, then, we have not only the possibility of making very short sentences, now we can make sentences as long as we want by a few added rules.

We have been thinking about a very simple language, the language PC. And, thus far we have confined ourselves to the syntax of this language. *Syntax* is the study of language from a purely formal point of view with no attention to meaning. If we were to talk about a natural language, we could go on and say a great deal about the language from this purely formal point of view. Some linguists in our century seem to imply that this is all there is to say, that the only important thing about language is the network of formal relationships and contrasts that exist in the language. In the United States, some of the most influential linguists before Chomsky seemed to have this idea. One was Leonard Bloomfield, another was Zellig Harris, who was Chomsky's teacher. Of course, they recognized that words have meanings, but they seemed to think that the study of meaning could not be done in a precise and scientific way. In this respect, they agreed with many philosophers and logicians who said that natural languages are so vague and ambiguous that they cannot be described in the same way that artificial languages, such as PC, can be described.

One philosopher who did not agree with this view was Richard Montague. In Montague's papers on natural language, which were written in the late 1960s and early 1970s, Montague claimed that natural languages could be treated in just the same way as the formal artificial languages of the logician. We may state this as a second thesis. I said something about Chomsky's thesis before. This is what I like to call "Montague's Thesis": Natural languages can be described as interpreted formal systems. Remember, I said Chomsky's thesis was that natural languages can be described as formal systems. Montague added to this the idea that natural languages can be described as interpreted formal systems. Montague took over from the logical tradition, the philosophical tradition, the methods of so-called model-theoretic semantics. This is the view I mentioned. Semantics assigns to sentences and other expression interpretations that are something other than language, in particular, it assigns to sentences the interpretations that have to do with whether they are true or false. In general, to determine whether a sentence is true or false, two things are necessary: (1) you must know what the sentence means and (2) you must face the sentence with some situation in the real world and see whether it corresponds to the meaning of the sentence.

(By the way, we can now see that the term *formal semantics,* which is used in the general title of these lectures, is quite misleading. The most essential thing about model-theoretic semantics is that it is not just about relations among expressions in some language or languages, but about relations between language and nonlanguage. The way in which the word *formal* is used in the term *formal semantics,* it means instead something similar to *explicit* or *precise.* Another footnote on that title: *informal* is intended to mean something like this: *without undue use of strange formalism.* A point I hope you will come to appreciate is that you can be quite precise in ordinary language. A formalism should pay for itself in increased perspicuity and understanding; it is not an end in itself.)

Now I want to take our simple language, PC, and show how we might go about giving an interpretation to this language by telling what the different kinds of expression in the language denotes. What we had before was the *syntax.* Now I am going to say something about the *semantics* of this language, something about the denotations of the different kinds of expression. And what I say is this: the terms denote individuals, the one-place predicates denote sets of individuals, the two-place predicates denote sets of pairs of individuals, and the formulas denote what I call truth-values. We will write *1* for True and *0* for False.

(You may think that the idea of letting the denotation of a predicate be a set is not very intuitive. Maybe *Walk* should rather mean something like the property of walking. If you think this, you are not alone. In later lectures I return to that idea. What we are looking at here is a standard theory about the denotations of a language developed by logicians and mathematicians who like to use *set theory* as a basic tool. It is a nice and well-understood theory and that is part of its appeal. But is has some drawbacks, as we will see. Similar remarks could be made about the idea of truth-values as the denotations of formulas.)

It is very important to understand what I am saying. What I am talking about here are these things in the world or in a model for the language which the different kinds of expressions in the language are supposed to refer to. So, think of a particular individual constant as having a person or a tea cup or a table as its semantic value or denotation. Here is a language, and here I am talking about a world of individuals and sets of individuals and pairs of individuals:

Now, before going on to say exactly how this all works, we need to think a little bit about the two kinds of terms: *individual constants* and *variables.* I said that they both denote individuals but they do it in a quite different way, and I have to spend a little time explaining that. The easiest thing is to think of individual constants as being like proper names in a language. So, these individual constants in this language, PC, work like *Emmon* or *Tom* or *John* or *Harry,* but we imagine that we can give names to many, many different kinds of things. So they always stand for some particular individual or thing. (For the time being, assume that constants—

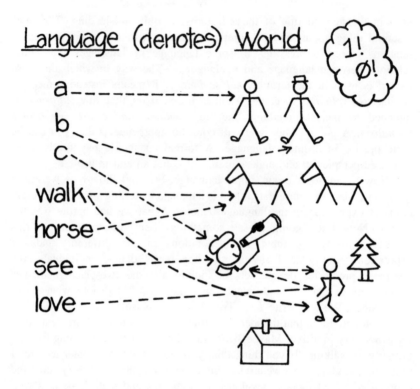

unlike real names in natural languages—always pick out a unique thing to which they refer. Consequently, you could think of each name as including a sort of *Universal Identification Number*.)

What about variables? Here we have to say that what variables denote depends on something that is called an *assignment of values to variables*. A variable is like a pronoun. So, variables work in this language very much like words, like *he, she,* or *it,* in a natural language like English. If we have a natural language sentence such as, "she is wise," how can we tell whether it is true or false? Well, we cannot determine its truth value unless we know who we are intending to mean by *she*. Therefore, part of the interpretation is an assignment of values to variables. And these assignments will always provide some particular individual for whatever variable we use, so that constants work like names and variables very much like variables in mathematics. A formula such as *Run(x)* cannot be judged true or false unless we know what individual is referred to by the variable. Therefore, we must have, in addition to what we have talked about already, an assignment of values or meanings to variables. Individual constants denote individuals very much like proper names do. Variables denote individuals under an assignment of values to the variables.

Now, you will notice that this language is extremely limited thus far because we do not yet have any way of making general statements. We can only say things such as :"John runs," or "Mary runs," or "It is happy." We have no way of saying things such as: "Someone is happy," or "Everyone is sad," and so on. Furthermore, stating that these words denote particular individuals, as our constant terms do, would not make sense. Who is *everyone* or *someone?* There are no general expressions in the language, and we need to add two more things to be able to say things of this more general nature. Again, I first give the syntax of these new expressions and then describe their meanings. So, to the definitions of formulas, I add a fifth rule:

R5. If *x* is a variable and *F* is a formula, then
    $\forall x\ F$ is a formula; and
    $\exists x\ F$ is a formula.

These are going to correspond to general statements that say:

Every *x* is an *F;* and

Some *x* is an *F*.

In the first formula, if we think about where the variable *x* appears in the formula, we make a general statement about everything, every individual in the interpretation. For the second, we make statements that correspond to English sentences such as "Someone runs." So, the first corresponds to a universal statement and the second to an existential sentence in logic. Now I have told you what kinds of denotations all of our expressions in this language have. Terms denote individuals. If they are constants, they are similar to names and denote particular individuals. If they are variables, like pronouns they denote individuals relative to a certain assignment of values to those variables. Predicates denote sets if they are one-place predicates. They denote sets of pairs of individuals, such as Mary and John, if they are two-place predicates. You must think of these pairs as ordered: Mary and (then) John is a different ordered pair from John and Mary. And all formulas denote truth-values: *1* for true and *0* for false.

To give the semantics for this language, I have to say something more about what particular denotations we assign to formulas on the basis of the denotations of their simpler parts. Consequently, what I have to do is give you a definition of what it is to be a true formula in this system. I think it would be best, in presenting this truth definition, not to give a precise definition I would have to write on the board and would look very complicated, but rather to look at some examples and see how we would go about defining the denotations of particular expressions in this language. Let me take some simple examples of expressions such as:

Run(a).

We want to determine when a formula like *Run(a)* is true and when it is false. On the one hand, we have the language, PC, and on the other hand, we have the world or model, and we want to ask about the formula: When are we going to say that this formula is true? Well, the semantic value, the denotation of the formula will equal *1* (True) just in case the individual denoted by *a* is in the set denoted by *Run*. So, when would the formula *Run(a)* be true? Well, we have to look at the world:

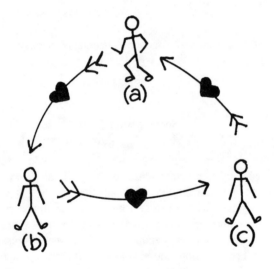

We find in this world the individual that *a* is supposed to denote. We find in the world a lot of other individuals who are running. There are many other things in the world—trees and pots and so on—but if the individual denoted by *a* is a member of the set of runners, then we say the formula is true. How would we define the truth conditions for *Love(a,b)*? Well, *look at the world again. We have to find some individual denoted by b* and let us say again we find the same individual for *a*. We now have to look at pairs of things in the model not just single things. Let us assume we have three things in our interpretation now: *A, B,* and *C.* and somehow we find the set of pairs that are in the denotation of *Love.* How we do that is not part of semantics, but somehow we know that A loves B. We will make a very sad story: A loves B. B loves C. And, C loves A. So this is the way the world is—we have a set of pairs—A + B; B + C; C + A—and then we ask about this formula: is it true? Well, it is true according to this world because in this world we said A does love B, so the formula is true. What about the formula *Love(b,a)?* According to what I have said here, this formula is false. Because B unfortunately does not love A. B loves C. And if we write that out, we would say: this formula is true just in case—exactly under the circumstance, or if and only if—the pair of individuals A and B are in the set of pairs that are the denotation of *Love* in this model. So this gives us a beginning point towards defining True and False with respect to a certain world or model. Notice one thing about what I have just said: I assume that the specification of the interpretation gives us complete information about all the individuals, sets, and so on, that we need to give denotations to the formulas of the language being interpreted. It is only on this understanding that we can conclude, for example, that B does not love A. In later lectures, we will take up the problem of dealing with a less idealized setup, where we might have only incomplete information.

(In this example, I have slipped over a general convention that I will try to follow: I cannot hand you real things in a model, as I sometimes draw pictures. But pictures are not very convenient either, so I've used uppercased letters, such as A, B, C, to correspond to the things denoted by the constants in our language, *A* for the thing that *a* denotes, and so on.)

Now, what about the other ways of forming formulas? You may remember one of the rules stated that if we have a formula, we can make another formula by putting the sign "-" in front of it:

$$-Love(b,a)$$

This sign is going to correspond to *not* or *negation*. When do we want this formula to be true? We want this formula to be true just in case the formula without the negation is false. So, we can say:

the denotation of *-Love(b,a)* = *1* (is true)

iff

the denotation of *Love(b,a)* = *0* (is false)

(*iff* is often used as an abbreviation for "if and only if".)

What about the formula:

$$(Run(a) \ \& \ Love(a,b))?$$

(The ampersand—&—corresponds to the word *and*.) And we want to say that this whole formula is true if and only if the first part is true *and* the second part is true. So that the formula

$$(Run(a) \ \& \ Love(a,b))$$

is true just in case the two individual parts are true. Is it true or is it not? It is true. I said before: *a* is one of the runners, *(a,b)* stands for one of the pairs that are in the denotation of *Love,* so because the first formula is true and the second formula is true, the whole thing is true. And this is what the denotations of such formulas are supposed to be.

Finally, for these simple examples: What about this formula?

$$((Run(a) \ \lor \ Love(a,b)))$$

Well, this formula is going to be true just in case either one of the component formulas is true. Thus, the sign & is like *and* and the sign ∨ is like *or*. And this formula will be true just in case (if and only if) either the first part is true or the second part is true or both of them are true. So again, given this model—Is the formula true?—does it denote *1* in this model? Yes, because both of the parts of it are true. It would also be true if one of them was false. Just as long as at least one of them is true, then the whole thing is true. It would be false only if both of the sides of the disjunction were false.

The only thing left to complete the semantics for language PC is to describe the denotations of formulas such as:

$$\forall x \ Run(x) \text{ and } \exists x \ Love(x,a).$$

Here we need to think a little bit about assignments of values of variables. And we want to say what the truth of the whole expression is on the basis of just the part without the quantifier in each case, and we need to say it in terms of assignments of values to variables. The whole formula (1) is going to be true if and only if (2)—what we get when we take away *Ax*—is true on every assignment of values to variables, that is, no matter what we take *x* to denote:

$$\text{the denotation of (1) } \forall x \ Run(x) \ = \ 1$$

iff

$$\text{the denotation of (2) } Run(x) \ = \ 1 \text{ on } every \text{ assignment of values to variables.}$$

For this example, this statement is correct. Some complications arise from the fact that we do not know whether there are other variables in the formula or not, if we do not know about the internal structure of the inner formula, but, for this particular formula which has only the one relevant variable x in it, this statement works (I return to this point in the next lecture). You might guess now what is going to happen with the other formula, the existential sentence. Again, we need to say what the truth condition is for the whole formula is on the basis of the truth of the inner formula, what we get when we strip off $\exists x$. You need to say what the whole thing will denote on the basis of just what the second part will denote and here we will say this:

the denotation of $\exists x \, Run(x) = 1$

iff

the denotation of $Run(x) = 1$ on *some* assignment of values to variables.

Thus, in the first case no matter how we assign values, we have to get a true formula. Say we have the variable x. One assignment would say that x denotes this person. Another assignment would say x denotes that person. Another assignment would say x denotes that thing. For the universal quantifier: If for *every* assignment of values to x the formula is true, then the whole thing is true. For the existential quantifier: If on *some* assignment—at least one assignment—of values to variables the formula is true, then the whole thing is true.

So that, in a very rapid form, is the theory of quantification. If this is the first time you have heard such an explanation and you understood it, you should be very proud because it took logicians a very long time to develop this theory of quantification in all its complexities. If this is the first time you have heard it and you feel that you don't quite understand it—if you feel as though you need to think about it a little more and play with it to understand it—then you're perfectly justified. It is a complex thing, and I am presenting it in far too rapid a manner. I do not want to say too much about formal technical details. I want to give you the basic idea so that we can then talk about the general issues that these lectures are aimed at.

What I have just been going through is really a restricted version of the so-called predicate calculus, which is a formal logical system, and I have given you an interpretation. The way that we have done this is an example of the general approach of a model-theoretic interpretation. I have been talking about a world or model and a language and a relationship between that language and the world in terms of denotations or meanings of expressions of this predicate calculus or PC.

The set of objects—or whatever it is we have in the model—I call a *model structure*. We have seen an example of a model structure for a particular language. One of the recurring questions and perhaps the main question of these lectures is: What kinds of model structures are most appropriate and revealing for studying the semantics of natural languages? not languages like PC, the predicate calculus, but English, Chinese, Russian, Thai, or whatever. What sorts of model structures do we want to set up if we want to try to pursue the semantics of natural languages in a model-theoretic manner? We will be studying various kinds of model structures for natural and artificial languages.

I would like to take a few minutes before we stop to say something about what we find in natural language that PC is not really able to cope with. The predicate calculus PC is too simple a system, and the model structure for it is too simple to be adequate for natural languages. Let me give you just a few examples of the way PC differs from a language like Chinese, or a language like English, by showing you what kinds of things we do not have.

In the parts of speech of PC, we have only three kinds of expressions — well, four maybe. We have terms, individual constants and variables, predicates of two kinds, and then we have things like *and* and *or* and parentheses and the universal quantifier and the existential quantifier, but we have only a very small number of kinds of expressions or parts of speech in PC. For natural language this won't do. We need more different kinds of expressions. For example, take a sentence such as, "John runs slowly." What is *slowly*? Nothing in PC corresponds to the adverb *slowly*. You have only predicates and individual terms. We can say something like, "John runs," but we can't say anything like, "John runs slowly." Or take an English sentence like, "Mary ran," as opposed to, "Mary runs." In English, of course, we must make an explicit choice of tense, and "Mary ran," does not mean the same thing as, "Mary runs." PC has nothing that corresponds to tense in natural language.

Or take a sentence such as, "Mary can run." We can only deal in PC with, "Mary runs," or "Mary does not run." What does it mean to say something like "Mary can run," or "It is possible that Mary will run."? Nothing corresponds to auxiliaries or moods, like subjunctives, words such as *can, should, may, must,* and so on. And PC does not have expressions of this sort. Natural languages do. We need to know something about how to have that sort of system in a model theory for natural language. We have no way of expressing conditionals. Sentences such as, "When it rains, it pours," or "If it is a nice day tomorrow, we will go to the beach," and so on. We have no way of connecting sentences with *if* or *when* yet. That is an easy thing to add. I will show you how to do that next time.

Furthermore, we do not have anything in this language that corresponds to what we need to interpret a sentence such as: "I live here." We can say, maybe, "John lives in Tianjin." We could say *live in* is a predicate and then *John* and then *T* or something for *Tianjin*, but we cannot say anything in this language like, "I live here." Now what does, "I live here," mean? *I* means me, but only if I am the one who is speaking. If you say, "I live here," then it means someone else. This language has no way of dealing with expressions that are determined by context. And, likewise, *here;* what does *here* mean? If I'm here, in this room, *here* might refer to this room. But if someone else says this sentence in another city, in another room then *here* in that sentence means something different. So, we need to think about context dependent words such as *I, here, now,* and so on.

In this language, we have no way of making complex sentences such as, "We will try to please you." That is where one sentence is somehow a component part of another sentence in a way that is not expressible in terms of simple *and, or, not,* and so on. Everything is a statement: John runs. Mary lives in Tianjin. Bill loves Sally. And so on. In this language, we have no way of asking questions. "Who lives in that house?" We have no way of making requests in PC. A language like PC, therefore, is very much limited to making statements about things and not asking questions or making requests, such as, "Please give me the time," and so.

The most important new thing we will be thinking about as we go along is the fact that in our interpretation of PC we thought only in terms of a single world or model. And, as we go along we will want to think about ways in which we can have a whole class of different models and think about the truth of sentences given different models. So that we will be able to think about possible different ways in which the world might be, rather than always in terms of a single actual model. And that brings in the notion of another possible world, which is simply a way in which things might be, not necessarily the way things are. We need this addition to our theory to be able to deal with sentences such as, "Mary can walk in the park." When is it true to say that Mary can walk in the park? Well, one way to answer that question is to say, "Mary can walk in the park," is true in this world if there is some other possible world, some other possible way in which thing might be, in which Mary does walk in the park. So we can explain modalities in terms of different ways in which the world might be. That will be the main topic of my next lecture.

Lecture II:

WORLDS ENOUGH
AND TIME

What I would like to do today is, first of all to spend some time reviewing part of what I said last time, especially the more technical details. Then I would like to address a topic I briefly introduced in my first lecture, that is, the idea of possible worlds.

In the first lecture I tried to give some first answers to the following question: What is model-theoretic semantics? I introduced the idea that a natural language may be treated as a formal system according to what I called Chomsky's Thesis, and added to that the idea that a natural language may be treated as an interpreted formal system (Montague's Thesis). This was the first step in answering the question about the nature of model-theoretic semantics. I then gave an example of a simple artificial language, PC. I talked about the syntax of this language and the semantics of this language. What I am raising really in all of these lectures is the following question: What kind of model structure is appropriate or adequate for natural language?

This is a theme to which we will return again and again. Before I go on any further, we might notice that this question presupposes a certain kind of answer because I have written here "natural language," as if all natural languages were the same with respect to the kind of model structure that they need. That is a very important and big question. We cannot simply assume that it is correct. But one hopes that just as in syntax where we try to develop a general theory of universal grammar within which we can account for the unity and the diversity of natural languages, in semantics also we look for a universal theory within which we can understand individual natural languages like Chinese, English, Amharic, Hindi, and so on. And so, the general thrust of the investigation is exactly the same here as it is in other parts of theoretical linguistics. So this formulation here has buried in it a certain goal or a certain assumption or hypothesis about all natural languages, namely that we can find an answer to this question that is universal and general in the same way that the universal theory of syntax allows us to account for the similarities and differences among different natural languages such as Chinese and English and so on. To illustrate these two points, I briefly talked about a certain formal language, which I called PC. PC is a part of what is called predicate calculus in logic. We looked at a very simple syntax for this language and then proceeded to interpret the syntax by telling what kind of a model structure is needed to interpret PC.

At the very end of the lecture, I began to ask the question: Is the model structure that we have looked at for PC adequate for a natural language as well? And I suggested that it was not. We will continue to look back at the simple system and see what it is that we have to do to a system of that sort to be able to get more and more adequate theories for the natural languages. Why are we looking at PC? Well, first, it is a very important language to know about if you are interested in logic. We know a great deal about both the syntax and the semantics of a simple system like this. Logicians and mathematicians like this language. They use it again and again. It has certain very nice properties. It is the most important language for the branch of mathematics known as *model theory*. Consequently, it is important to understand that this is not simply an arbitrary example I chose, but it is significant in its own right if you wish to continue to study logic as part of the understanding of natural language.

Now, let me first say that the PC that I presented is only a part of predicate calculus. The only thing that forces me to say that this is a part of predicate calculus is that we have restricted ourselves to one-place and two-place predicates. Remember the simple formulas:

$$Run(x) \text{ and } Love(a,b).$$

The predicate calculus as a full system continues to add predicates of as many places as you want. For example, it will have things corresponding to English words like *give:* A gives B to C; so we can have three-place relations in predicates. We can have four-place relations in predicates: A buys B some C for D. This is an inessential restriction for our purposes here. So, it is only in this sense that I have been talking about a subpart of the predicate calculus. All the important things are there.

Let me briefly outline without laying out in detail what we have had in our version or fragment of predicate calculus. We have the following kinds of expressions: terms, that is, individual variables and constants. The reason why we must say *individual* constants and variables will become clear later when we look at richer systems of the sort that we need to deal with natural language. Then we had predicates, one-place, two-place. And, as I just mentioned, now the full predicate calculus would just continue with predicates of as many places as you wish—as a logical system. We have a definition of formula. Formulas were introduced by describing ways to combine predicates and terms as in the examples above, and we had ways of making disjunctions *(or)* and conjunctions *(and)* and negations *(not)*. In addition, we had quantifiers, the universal quantifier and the existential quantifier, which I am writing like this:

$$\forall x \text{ and } \exists x.$$

This is the syntax of PC: terms: two kinds; predicates: two kinds; formulas: simple formulas formed by taking predicates together with terms, more complex ones made by using quantifiers, negations, and connectors. And, remember, when we use either of the two connectors (& and v), we put parentheses around the result so it is clear what was connected. Let me illustrate why this is important. Suppose we say that p, q, and r are formulas. There is a crucial difference between saying

$$((p \ \& \ q) \lor r)$$

and saying

$$(p \ \& \ (q \lor r)).$$

(They will have different truth conditions, as you can check for yourselves.) This is why we need parentheses around our complex formulas. (If you read other logic books, you will find a variety of different symbols for the things I have introduced here.)

Another small footnote about a system of this sort: I have given you almost all the connectives that are standardly used in the predicate calculus and in the calculus of sentence meanings or propositional calculus. It is possible, if one is a logician and interested in such things, to take only a very few of these as primitive and define all of the others. I have not done that, however; this is not a logic course. Very often you will see a definition of a predicate calculus that has only these signs as primitives: &, −, ∃, or v, −, ∃. And then some definitions will give you all of the others.

I also talked about an *interpretation* or *semantics*. I call it the standard interpretation of a language like PC. What is an *interpretation?* Well, I have said a little about that already; let me repeat it again. An *interpretation,* in the sense of a model-theoretic theory of semantics, is some way of assigning denotations in a certain model structure to expressions in a language. So, an interpretation of a language has two parts. The first part is what I have called a *model structure,* which is simply the kinds of things needed to interpret the language. In the standard interpretation of the predicate calculus, exactly two kinds of things are needed, because it is a very, very simple system. All you need is a set, which I call E, of individuals and a set of truth values. No standard way of naming that set exists, but it is just a set that I wrote as *1* and *0*. Consequently, two truth values and a set of individuals are the standard model structure for the predicate calculus.

I also said something last time about the way these things are connected to the expressions by means of the interpretation. This is the second thing that we need: a way of assigning elements in the model structure to the expressions of the language. As you recall, when we have terms, these terms are connected directly to the set of individuals if they are constants, or they are connected indirectly to the set of individuals according to an assignment of values to variables.

We saw that we can use a certain model structure to define the way we interpret predicates. One-place predicates are simply interpreted as sets of individuals. So, something within the entire set of individuals might be the interpretation of a predicate like *Run,* it is the individuals that run. But in the interpretation of two-place predicates, we needed to have not *single* individuals but *pairs* of individuals. A person who loves another person. A pair ordered in a certain way. And if we continued with this, we simply take pairs (two-tuples of individuals), triples, ordered four-tuples of individuals, and so on. But, as I said, all we need to think about are one-place and two-place predicates.

So, what is an *interpretation?* An *interpretation,* thus far, needs three things. First, it needs a certain model structure—let us call this model structure *M1. M1* is the first simple model structure that we are looking at. *M1* is the model structure of a standard interpretation of the predicate calculus. In addition to this, two things are needed: one, a set (called G) of assignments of values to variables, and we need a certain evaluation function which I will call D. This is the *evaluation function* or *mapping* or *procedure*—a way of taking expression of the language and saying what they are supposed to mean or denote within this model structure. Consequently, these three things are part of the standard interpretation of the predicate calculus: a certain model structure, a certain set of assignment of values to variables, and an evaluation function. The following is a summary of the interpretation's structure:

$$<M1, D, G>.$$

What does D mean? D is just a shorthand way of saying such and such denotes such and such. So, if I say, as I said last time, that the predicate *Run* denotes a set of individuals, a shorthand way of saying this is:

$$D(Run) = \text{the set of individuals that run.}$$

Or, we can say things like this:

$$D(b) = \text{a certain individual, say Bill, in the model.}$$

Thus, to repeat, the evaluation function is simply a way of assigning elements of the model to expressions of the language.

Now, I want to spend some time talking about the assignment of values to variables because it is a rather tricky point which we must be clear; it will help us understand what we are doing.

How do assignments of values to variables fit into all of this? For the interpretation of constant symbols, we do not need to refer to assignments at all. But for the interpretation of formulas that have variables in them, the assignment functions are quite crucial. We need them for what are called *open formulas* (or *sentences*), first of all, because without an assignment we do not know what to do with a formula such as *Run(x)*. Here we will say that the formula is true on a particular assignment g of values to variables—that is, it denotes I—just in case the thing assigned to x by g is in the set of runners. We write the name of that individual like this: $g(x)$. So, when I am talking about the denotation function D, in general, I am talking about the denotation with respect to some g in the set of assignments G, which can be written: D_g.

Because we define the truth of formulas with existential or universal quantifiers on the basis of the open formula we get by stripping off the quantifier ($\forall x$ or $\exists x$, for example), the assignments are a very crucial part of the definition of truth in our theory. To say this very carefully, we have to worry about whether the formula with which we are dealing has other free variables in it besides the one bound by the quantifier. So, a full statement of the truth definition for the universal quantifier has to be given thusly:

$\forall x\, F$ denotes I on an assignment g iff F denotes I on every assignment g', which is just like g except possibly at the value that g' assigns to x.

Let me go through the way this works.

If x is the only free variable in F—for example, if the formula is *Run(x)*—then we would not have to worry about the part of the definition that talks about assignments similar to the one we started with (the "except possibly . . ." part). But suppose it is not; suppose we have a formula such as *See(x,y)*. Then the point of the complicated clause comes out: we want just to think about assignments that agree on the value they assign to y. And we need to let them be different just for the special case of *x:* that is what the "possibly different" part of the definition is intended to take care of. So much for assignments.

The first possible answer to the main question we are raising might then be this: *M1* is a possible model structure for natural language semantics. *M1* was not conceived of as a model structure for natural language but for a simple but very important formal language, and one of our first questions will be: How adequate is such a model structure for a natural language? And we will ask this repeatedly about the different model structures that we look at.

What I would like to do for the rest of the session today is to elaborate on what I just mentioned last time and try to make clear the notion of a possible world that arises when we begin to ask about the adequacy of a system of this sort for natural language. Before I do that, however, let me make a couple of clarifications about just what it is that we are doing here. I said that the task of a model-theoretic semantics is to provide a way of associating expressions of a language with denotation and in particular to give a theory of truth for that language. We must be very clear about one thing—that we are engaged in logic for linguistics, but we are not engaged in science in general. It is not part of our job to be able to decide when particular statements are true or false about the real world. It is not part of linguistics to say whether Einstein's theory of relativity or Newton's theory of mechanics is a correct theory about the world. It is not part of semantics to determine when it is true that I am intelligent or stupid or something similar. We are concerned here with the form of truth, not with how we find out whether something is true; we are not concerned with the theory of knowledge, in other words, a way of finding out truth; we are concerned merely with the structure of the theory of truth which begins by saying something like: Given that it is true that such and such, then it must be true that such and such. We are not concerned with the ultimate, and very important, question: How do we know whether something is true? In philosophy, it is called the *theory of knowledge* or *epistemology;* or, one could say that it is simply science or how we know about what is true in the world. We are concerned with the structure of an interpretation rather than the basis for it.

Let us now continue with the question, "How adequate is this sort of a picture for natural language?" One thing I mentioned last time is that natural languages seem to have many more different kinds of words than the kinds of words that we have here. We not only have things that look like predicates— that is, verbs of various kinds—and pronouns and names and things like that, but we also have many other kinds of expressions in a natural language which seem to have no counterpart here in the predicate calculus. I will address that question in more detail but not right now. I mentioned briefly last time that adverbs such as *slowly* do not exist in a system of this sort. No prepositions are found in a system of this sort. Next time—we will barely touch on this today—I will ask about some particular parts of speech, how natural languages are able to build complex expressions that correspond to our simple expression in the language of this sort. There are, so to speak, two grammatical differences between PC and a natural language. First, many more kinds of words and expressions are found in natural language than are found in the predicate calculus. That is a syntactic question: however, it is also a semantic question because we want to know the corresponding meanings for these different kinds of expressions. Second, in the predicate calculus only very simple predicates, such as *Run, Love, See,* and so on are found. We know that in natural languages we can have very complex phrases that correspond to simple predicates like *Run,* and we need to spend some time thinking about that.

What I want to concentrate on now is a fundamental change that comes about when we begin to ask about some different kinds of sentences. Suppose we have sentences like these:

1. Mary can speak English.
2. John could wash the dishes.
3. Necessarily, 2 + 2 = 4.

Notice that these sentences have certain words in them that do not seem to fit the categories found in PC, either an adverb *(necessarily)* or words we think of as auxiliaries in English. I guess in Chinese a class of words of this sort is also found, which are somehow concerned with the whole meaning of the sentence but do not seem to be sentences of the sort that we can deal with adequately in the standard interpretation of the predicate calculus. Why is that the case? As I suggested last time, it is because nothing in this model structure or in the evaluation function or in the assignment is found that allows us to talk about different possible circumstances, different possible ways in which things might be. In other words, the standard interpretation of the predicate calculus assumes a certain fixed model that does not change. One is always giving an interpretation of the language under consideration in a fixed single model, a fixed single set of individuals, two truth values, and so on, as the full interpretation. But it seems as if in a sentence like number 3 we are making a much larger statement. We are not just saying that in the actual world, in a single model that we are using to interpret the language, 2 + 2 = 4. What does it mean to say, "Necessarily, 2 + 2 = 4"? Well, one answer to that question was given by logicians who developed a number of systems called *modal logics,* to come to understand in logical systems what *logical truth, necessarily true,* and so on mean. The first interpretations of systems of modal logic were developed in the 1960s by a number of logicians, but probably the most well-known logician was Saul Kripke. He used the notion of a possible world to come to understand what sentences like number 3 mean. I want to spend the remainder of the session on that idea. The main topic today, then, is possible worlds.

What I will talk about from now on today is a certain kind of model-theoretic semantics that makes use of the notion of a possible world. Possible world semantics is a certain subtheory, a certain kind of model-theoretic semantics and is not to be identified with model-theoretic semantics itself. I say that because very often in the literature, you will read statements about model-theoretic semantics that make the mistake of thinking that possible world semantics is the only type of model-theoretic semantics that exists. This is just one particular type of model-theoretic semantics, which is perhaps the most well understood and most well developed, but it is certainly not the only kind of model-theoretic semantics that exists. Next week, we'll be looking at some slightly different systems that are not really systems of possible world semantics at all. Richard Montague's interpretations of English, Montague's most important papers on English semantics, did use possible world semantics.

Let us pretend now that we have extended our PC to include expressions of the sort that are supposed to correspond to words like *necessarily*. So we want to say: What does "Necessarily, F" mean, where F is a formula. Or, more concretely, we need to say: Under what conditions would we say that "Necessarily, $2 + 2 = 4$" is true? The answer that you might expect given the general form that our explanations have taken so far is to say under what conditions F or "$2 + 2 = 4$" is to be true:

$$\text{Necessarily } F = 1 \text{ iff } ? \, F = 1$$

Notice that this is the general technique of trying to deal with complex expressions in this language. We discuss the meaning for $Ax \, F$ in terms of the interpretation of just the simple part without the quantifier. Here we are asking the question: What do we need to say about when "Necessarily F" is true in terms of when F is true?

The answer is that "Necessarily F" is true if and only if in every possible world F is true. Now we cannot say that in the apparatus of the system that we have in the standard interpretation of the predicate calculus. Why can't we say that? Because all we have here are individual and truth-values in the model structure. We cannot talk about different ways in which a world might be. And possible world semantics simply adds to this standard interpretation a new set of elements. The new set of elements is a set of possible worlds. The new model structure has, again, a set of individuals, again, a set of truth-values and we add, now, a new set of things W, a set of possible worlds:

$$\begin{array}{cc} \text{M1: E} & \text{M2': E} \\ \{0, 1\} & \{0, 1\} \\ & W \end{array}$$

(Curly braces are used to enclose sets, thus { 0, 1} means the set consisting of 0 and 1. I call this new model *M2'* because soon I will revise it slightly and I want to reserve *M2* for the revised version.) Now, let us add a new example, and see if we can guess what the answer might be given the new possibility of talking about possible worlds. Suppose we wanted to understand a sentence like this:

4. Possibly, it is raining in Beijing.

We want to say when it is true to say that it is possibly raining in Beijing. Our suggestion is going to be very much like what we have said about example number 3. Sentence 4 is true just in case in some possible world it is actually true in that world that it is raining in Beijing. So a possible world is really not very mysterious. It is simply a way of thinking about ways in which the world might be different from the way it actually is.

Let me offer another example. Suppose we were sitting around after dinner in someone's house — there was someone there named John and someone says the sentence, "Well, John could wash the dishes." Under what conditions could we say that is true in that situation. Well, we could say that is true in that situation or world if there is some possible world in which "John is washing the dishes" is true. Or, what about "Mary can speak English." We must not worry too much at this point about the exact understanding of these things, because there are many complicated and difficult questions about what a word like *can* really means in a natural language like English. But, following the same style of presentation, suppose I see someone named Mary here, and I say, "Well, Mary can speak English." Mary may be, at the moment, sleeping or reading a book or talking to someone in some other language, Chinese perhaps. What I would be saying according to this manner of explaining modality, of explaining modal ideas like *can* and *must* and *should* and so on would be something like saying, "Mary can speak English" is true if there is some possible world in which Mary does speak English or is speaking English right now.

You might notice here a rather elegant parallel between the simple language PC with its model structure *M1* and the new model structure *M2'* (and languages for which it is designed). PC has two kinds of quantification over individuals, corresponding to *all* and *some*. Our new kind of structure involves the same two kinds of quantification over individuals, corresponding to *all* and *some*. Our new kind of structure involves the same two kinds of quantification, but now over worlds rather than individuals.

For the first answer to the fundamental question, "What kind of model structure is adequate for natural language?" we looked at the simple interpretation of the predicate calculus. What I am beginning now is to demonstrate how this model structure, this interpretation system, is not adequate for natural language and to try to show some of the ways in which we can enrich this kind of interpretation to approach a system that is adequate for natural language. The first addition is to say: let us look at a system slightly more complicated, slightly richer than the standard interpretation, by adding a certain set of things called possible worlds.

Let me give another kind of example. Suppose we have a sentence like this:

5. John should not walk in the park.

We want to understand what sentence 5 means on the basis of what sentence 6 means:

6. John does not walk in the park.

What does it mean to say "John should not walk in the park" in this world? What I am saying suggests that the answer lies in thinking about other possible worlds. Sentence 5 is true just in case in all of the "should worlds," all of the worlds that should be the case, John does not walk in the park. In fact, perhaps, John is walking in the park. We want to say, well, it is true that John is walking in the park but in some other kind of circumstance, namely, the kind of circumstance that should be the case, John is not walking in the park, so that possible worlds have to do with understanding alternative ways in which things might be. And this is all that the phrase *possible worlds* means.

I am going to add another thing to our kind of model structure and then we will have everything needed for Montague's full theory of the semantics for English. What I want to add deals with the interpretation of sentences like:

7. Mary is walking in the park.

Suppose we consider different versions of the sentence that come about when we vary the tense/aspect part of the sentence, leaving everything else constant:

8. Mary walked in the park.
9. Mary has walked in the park.
10. Mary will walk in the park.
11. Mary will have walked in the park.

Many of you are teachers of English, and one of the things you have to teach your students is how the tense system of English works, which is quite different from Chinese, as I understand it. We need, in an adequate theory of natural language, to deal with variations of this sort, and it appears as if we have nothing yet so far in our model structure to deal with differences of tense. But in a sense we already do, because the notion of a possible world by itself could include the idea of the same world at different times. So that we could simply take the set of possible worlds and think about a certain ordering in time and use this notion also to understand systems of tense. We say that "Mary walked in the park," is true at a certain world if there is an earlier world—a world that is ordered earlier in relation to the present world—and in that earlier world, "Mary walks in the park," is true. So, in a sense, the notion of possible worlds already has in it the possibility to talk about relationships of time. But it is convenient, and this is what Montague did in his fragment, to add a different set of things, a set of times, to our model structure, together with a certain ordering of the elements of this new set. So we have a set of worlds and now a set of times. Let us look and see how that might work here to deal with tense.

We want to understand what a sentence such as, "Mary will walk," means, considering that as a simple future in English. Here, we want to take the future *will* out of the sentence, leaving the simple sentence, "Mary walks," in the present tense, and we want to say what the meaning of the first sentence is, when it is going to be true in terms of what the conditions are for the second sentence to be true:

12. Mary will walk in the park.
13. Mary walks in the park.

Now you might guess what the answer will be. Sentence 12 will be true at a certain time, t, if and only if there is a later time, t', at which sentence 13 is true. What do I mean by *later?* I mean that t' is *after* now. So our model structure includes not just a set of possible worlds but a set of times with an ordering given on them. And I think you can see how we can go ahead to talk about the truth of, "Mary has walked," or "Mary walked."

Introducing these fundamental changes into the model structures we are using to interpret natural languages brings with it an important change in our ideas about what a meaning is. In talking about the way *M1* can be used to interpret PC, we said that the meaning of our expressions could be thought of as individuals and sets, sets of pairs, and so on. With the introduction of possible worlds and times we have implicitly added something crucially different in our attempt to understand what a meaning is. Because an interpretation is now given relative to a world (or a world and a time) we must have meanings with the power to look at different worlds and times and *find* the kinds of things we had in *M1:* individuals, sets, sets of pairs, and so on. I will return to this point in later lectures, because it is a very significant part of the kind of semantic theory we are looking at.

In a short time, I have given you the basic notion of possible worlds and times, and these correspond to two very well-developed branches of logic called *modal logic* and *tense logic*. Richard Montague, who I am following here, knew these two systems of logic or families of systems of logic very well, and he used them to interpret English. So here really is Montague's answer to the question, "What do we need for an adequate model structure for a natural language?" And Montague said that we need at least this much. Thus, Montague's answer to the question, "What do we need to interpret English?" was, this sort of a model structure—again, together with an evaluation function and set of assignments to variables—and it differs from the standard model structure and the standard interpretation of the predicate calculus only in the addition of these two new things: a set of possible worlds and set of times. If you take a look at the best-known paper of Montague's, his so-called *PTQ*, you will see I have given you exactly what Montague said in this basic paper.

(Montague wrote three basic papers about the interpretation of natural language. *PTQ* is the best known one. If you take a look at the introduction to Montague semantics done by Dowty, Wall, and Peters (1981), you will find that almost the entire book is devoted to explaining *PTQ* in ordinary English (!). *PTQ* is only a little over 20 pages long. In this course, I have covered, very rapidly, about the first three chapters and a little bit of later chapters of the book by Dowty, Wall, and Peters.)

To summarize our new model structure, revised to make a distinction between worlds and times, looks like this:

$$M2 = \begin{array}{l} E\text{: a set of individuals} \\ W\text{: a set of possible worlds;} \\ T\text{: a set of times, with a certain ordering} \\ \quad \text{relation } \underline{R} \text{ on them; and} \\ \{1, 0\}\text{: the set of truth values.} \end{array}$$

So an interpretation, under this view, consists of the model structure $M2$, an interpretation function D and a set G of assignment of values to variables: $<M2, D, G>$.

I would like to add two footnotes to the picture I have just given of the model structure that Montague used in *PTQ*. The first has to do with the structure of times in the model, the second with some further aspects of possible worlds and modality. Let me stress, however, that what I have said really does exhaust what there is in that model structure. We will see in the next few lectures that quite a lot can be accomplished within this system in the way of interpreting natural language.

The set T of times (called J in *PTQ*) is given by Montague without any comment. We do not know whether it is supposed to be a set of dimensionless instants or intervals with some "thickness" to them, although from other writings of Montague we might guess that he meant the former. Much discussion has occurred about this point in the years since *PTQ* appeared, and I will return to this point in a later lecture. The relation R (called in *PTQ*) is pinned down to be what is called a simple ordering; that is, an ordering that is transitive, reflexive, and antisymmetric:

> *transitive:* if t is "before" t' and t' is "before" t'', then t is "before" t'';
> *reflexive:* every time t is "before" (or the same as) itself; and
> *antisymmetric:* if t is "before" t' and vice versa, then t is the same as t'.

(I've written "before" because we need to think of it as really meaning "before or simultaneous with" as is suggested by Montague's notation.)

About worlds: First, the setup in *M2* is about the simplest one possible. You can get from any world to any other world with no problems. More refined accounts are often used in which not only the times but also the worlds have certain specified relations among them, the so-called accessibility relations. In these systems, which have proved very fruitful for thinking about the semantics of conditional sentences, the definitions of necessity and the like are modified in such a way as to refer to worlds that are "accessible" to the one you start with. Different ways of spelling out these relationships lead to different systems of modal logic. Second, the system is very clean and simple in another way: there is presumed to be just one kind of necessity, possibility, and so on. In a broader perspective this does not seem quite right. Modal expressions sometimes seem to be referring to logical modality, sometimes to moral obligation or desirability, sometimes to physical possibility, and so on. For example, if I say, "You can't do that!" I might be trying to tell you any number of different things, depending on the context (trying to trisect an angle, build a perpetual motion machine, learn a new language in a week, treat an older person with disrespect, and so on). Consequently, a more refined and adequate way of dealing with natural language modality is to take these sorts of differences into account. (A hint of this way of thinking appeared above when I was speaking about "should worlds.")

I promised that in these lectures we would look at some issues of concern in current research in semantics and so far it seems as if I have concentrated mostly on the complicated, technical aspects. I would like to end this lecture, therefore, with a brief look at some fundamental issues that arise just with the apparatus I have touched on thus far. They are not new issues, but they continue to concern philosophers and linguists, and I think that they are interesting.

Individuals and Worlds. Suppose you are in one world and want to go to another one, in order, say, to interpret a conditional sentence like this one:

14. If Emily Dickinson had been born a man, she would probably not have been as great a poet.

In order to understand this sentence, we have to identify a certain individual in this other world as Emily Dickinson. Is he the *very same individual* in his other world? Notice that in English, we still use *she* to refer to *her* (*it? him?*). Montague followed this line, which has been argued for most forcefully by Kripke (1972). Another view (most vigorously defended by Lewis [1968], for example), is that each world comes furnished with its own set of individuals and that to understand a sentence like sentence 14 we have to appeal to a *counterpart* of Emily Dickinson in that other, counterfactual world.

Conditionals are just one example of what have been called *world-creating* contexts. Others include not only modals (as we have seen) but language about dreaming, imagining, wishing, trying, and so on. They all bring us issues about *transworld identification* (what David Kaplan, [I believe], dubbed "trans-world heir-lines"). One interesting problem that arises when discussing the issues of transworld identification is illustrated by a sentence like this one:

15. If I had really been twins, I would have been a lot happier!

As Lewis has pointed out, if we insist on real transworld identity, then we have to face the problem of how one thing can be two things!

Worlds and Times. In the model structure *M2* of *PTQ*, the set of times is completely independent of the set of worlds. This means we can always climb around from world to world and back and forth in time, carrying our watches so to speak, and coordinate in time what is happening in whatever world we are in with what is going on in all the other worlds. Is this right? Notice that if relativity theory is correct, then we cannot literally do this even in one world, our own one. People differ in their reactions to questions like this. Some say: Natural language was developed or evolved in a nicely local world where we did not have to worry about subtleties like this. Others, me among them, say: But we *use* natural language to reason about things like this, to develop theories about physics, and so on.

Issues like these illustrate an important conceptual problem: What is the status of the concepts that we use in our theories? Are we supposed to be making claims about the world? About the way we understand the world when we use language? Or what? While I do not have any answers to such questions, I think they are important questions, and I will return to them occasionally.

Lecture III:

NOUNS AND NOUN PHRASES

The title of today's lecture is taken from an article I published quite a few years ago. The paper was written when vigorous interactions among linguists, philosophers, and logicians were just beginning. In that paper, I argued that the basic logical structure of natural languages was very much like that of the artificial logical languages of writers like Tarski, Carnap, Reichenbach, and others; that is, basically, the kind of structure that we have looked at here under the name of PC. I now believe that view was quite inadequate. Probably, it was the result of my ignorance of just how rich the resources of modern logic are. Today, we will look in detail at the way one logician, Richard Montague, solved some of the hard problems that arise when you try to give a detailed and precise account of the syntax and semantics of a natural language such as English. But before I go into this, I would like to take up a couple of general issues that arise in trying to give precise interpretations to natural languages.

The first issue is that of *ambiguity*. The language PC is completely unambiguous. Given any well-formed formula in the language, it is possible to show that there is just one interpretation that can be assigned to the expression (ignoring for now the question of the possible assignments of values to variables). Natural languages are not like that. Many expressions —

perhaps *most* expressions—can have many different interpretations. These ambiguities can arise in a number of different ways.

In the first place, individual words that mean quite different things can sound exactly the same (or look exactly the same in written forms). Consider this sentence:

    1. John sat by the crane.

How could we possibly assign a truth-value (relative to a world and time) to this sentence? The word *crane* has two quite different meanings: a kind of large bird and a piece of machinery for lifting very large objects. Or, to say it differently, there are two words—*crane1* and *crane2*—which are pronounced (and spelled) just the same. So one kind of ambiguity just comes from the fact that natural languages in general seem to have lots of homonyms: different lexical elements that sound (or look) alike. Let us call this type of ambiguity *lexical ambiguity*. (It is a difficult question to decide when we have two different words and when we have one word used in different ways, with different senses, as in *I run, the machine runs,* and so on.)

[*Excursus on the Fundamental Nature of Linguistic Items.* It is easy to become confused about what the linguistic things or expressions are that we deal with when we want to talk precisely about language. We have to remind beginning students again and again that they should not identify words with their written form. As linguists, we have gotten used to the primary nature of speech (or sign in the languages of the deaf) in thinking about language. But we have our own traps. We cannot identify the phonological form of an expression with the expression itself. The Swiss linguist Ferdinand de Saussure was very clear about this: a linguistic *sign* is best thought of as a linking between sound and meaning. In more modern terms, we can think of a linguistic expression as a bundle of representations: *phonological, syntactic, semantic, morphological,* and maybe more. To help keep this fundamental idea straight, I often identify an expression with an arbitrary number, which you can think of as an address in some computational device. So, the English word that we spell *fish* is identified with, say, A237. Then, we say about A237 that it has such and such a phonological representation, such and such a bundle of syntactic properties, such and such a semantic interpretation and representation, and so on. In a way, the Chinese writing system models this kind of an idea more accurately—at least in idealized cases—than an alphabetic or syllabic system such as those of Finnish or Japanese. One part of a typical Chinese character often relates to the meaning of the item, another to the phonological ("phonetic") side of the item.]

But even when we have unambiguous words, or when we fix on one meaning for ambiguous words, cases are still found where the very same words arranged in the very same way seem to express different meanings and demand different accounts of their truth conditions. Let us consider an example that will be of some importance for one of today's main topics:

2. Every child was teasing a tiger.

English speakers agree that this sentence is ambiguous. We can make this ambiguity clear by considering two situations: in one, for each child under discussion there is at least one tiger that that child is teasing but there may be no one tiger that every child is teasing; in the other, there is at least one tiger that every child is teasing. (I am ignoring and will continue to ignore tenses today, for the most part.) Using the language PC, we can display these two interpretations as follows:

2'. $\forall x\ \exists y\ Tease(x, y)$.
2". $\exists y\ \forall x\ Tease(x, y)$.

(These formulas ignore the fact that we are talking about children and tigers, for simplicity's sake; thus, they really mean something like the meaning of the English sentence, "Everything was teasing something.") Let us call this type of ambiguity *structural ambiguity*.

What this example shows is that we cannot achieve an adequate model-theoretic semantics for English just by means of an evaluation function like *D* of the last lecture. A function is a mapping that must give us a unique value for each argument it is given. How are we to solve this problem?

There seem to be just two possibilities here. One is to give up the idea of a function that yields single denotations for natural language expressions. The other way is the one more usually followed: it is to set up some kind of representation of the different meanings or structures; that is, to provide a level of representation where these differences are displayed and to define the function *D* on *this* language, which must then be related to our original language (Chinese, English) in some way. Such a representation is sometimes called the *logical form* of the language, but I must warn you that this term is used in many different ways. We will follow this latter course for now, but return in a later lecture to the other option.

The other general issue I wish to raise is the question of *compositionality*. The idea here (often attributed to Gottlob Frege) is that it must be possible to figure out the meanings (in our terminology, the denotations) of complex expressions on the basis of the meanings (denotations) of the simpler expressions out of which they are constructed and the way in which they are put together. Our sample semantics for PC followed this principle of compositionality, as you can check for yourselves. A great deal is left to be said about this issue, but I will postpone more detailed consideration of the issues until later in the lectures. For now, let us just take note of a kind of paradox that arises when we think about ambiguity and compositionality.

It is a fact about the use of natural language that we do not usually notice ambiguities until they are pointed out to us or experience a failure of communication. The common sense answer to the question of how this can be so is this: usually the context (linguistic or actual) lets us know how we are to understand potentially ambiguous expressions. But this means that the meaning of the whole is not a function of the meaning of the parts! To obtain the meaning of the parts, we have to grasp the meaning of the whole and even the larger contexts in which the whole is used. Again, there are very difficult questions to face here, but I will not face them yet. For now, I just ask you to start to think about them. (Zhūang Zǐ thought about them when he asked: "How can words be so obscure and yet admit of right or wrong?")

Let me introduce the main topics of today's discussion by comparing the structure of PC, our simple starting language, with the kinds of systems we are more familiar with in natural languages. It is usual in both traditional and modern grammars to distinguish a number of different kinds of words or expressions—in modern usage they are called *categories,* in older terminology *parts of speech.* What do we find in PC?

We have seen that PC has two main kinds of simple expressions and one kind of complex expression. The former are *Predicates* (of various subtypes) and *Terms* (of two types). The one kind of complex expression is the *Formula,* divided into simple or *atomic* formulas and complex formulas. But there are other expressions in the language that, as yet, do not have their own categories; they are just introduced by way of rules: $-$, $\vee$, $\&$, $\forall$, $\exists$, $($, $)$.

Now let us compare PC to a natural language like English. First of all, in natural languages there are many more categories: nouns, noun phrases, verbs, verb phrases, adjectives, adjective phrases, articles, demonstratives, adverbs, prepositions and postpositions, sentences, and for each of these categories and others I have not mentioned various subtypes, not to speak of all the grammatical affixes, particles, and on and on.

Standard logic textbooks that try to provide some insight into the logical structure of natural languages (or try to help students understand logical systems by reference to natural language) often make identifications like these:

LOGIC	LANGUAGE
Formula	Sentence
Predicate	Verb
	Noun
	Adjective
Term	
Constant	Name
Variable	Pronoun

What about the remaining symbols, the ones that were introduced directly in our rules? (If you want a fancy term for such items, you can call them *syncategorematic elements*.) Some of them correspond to natural language categories, namely, conjunctions such as *and* and *or*. Others, the parentheses, do not, but they correspond to devices we use in grammatical descriptions of natural languages (tree diagrams, labelled bracketings). The remaining two—the universal and existential quantifier symbols ∀ and ∃—do not directly correspond to any natural language items. We will be taking up this discrepancy in some detail today. But let us observe that all of these extra symbols play somewhat the same role in PC as many of the elements of natural language that we consider part of the grammatical structure of the language: bound affixes, particles, and the like. I understand that a distinction is drawn in the Chinese linguistic tradition between *full words* and *empty words,* and this same sort of distinction is drawn in many linguistic traditions between *lexicon* and *grammar*. In practical terms, it is something like this: if I want to learn something about a new language, I will get myself both a grammar book and a dictionary, and I will expect to learn different kinds of things from these two sources.

There is one very obvious difference between natural languages and PC that I have not mentioned explicitly yet. In PC all of the content expressions ("full" expressions) are simple primitive symbols: predicates, individual constants (like names in natural languages) and variables (like pronouns). In natural languages, on the other hand, we can build up expressions or phrases that work like such simple primitive expressions and we can make them as long or complex as we like. Here are some examples of simple expressions and complex expressions that work logically like the simple ones:

3. Mary: the tall woman who is talking
4. walks: walks slowly in the park
5. everyone: whoever believes that linguistics is interesting

We want to see today how we can treat natural languages that have such complex representatives of the basic categories. We will concentrate on complex nouns and noun phrases.

Before going into details, there is one small thing that will be useful for us to discuss. I will introduce it first as an addition to PC. It is a way of connecting formulas in a way analogous to those we have in natural languages for joining sentences by means of words such as *imply* or locutions like *if . . . then:*

6. If it rains, then it pours.
7. If Socrates is a human and all humans are mortals, then Socrates is mortal.

In PC, we can introduce a new symbol and a corresponding meaning rule:

R7. If *F* and *G* are formulas, so is *(F → G)*.

S7. *(F → G)* is true iff *F* is false or *G* is true.

(From example S7 you can see that we can state the truth conditions for the formulas constructed with → in terms of negation and disjunction, that is, *not* and *or*. This relation is sometimes called *material implication* to emphasize that it is a technical concept and does not correspond exactly to the way we use *if . . . then* or *implies* in natural languages.) We will need this relation in order to see how to deal with the denotations of some noun phrases like *every fish*. (To complete things let me add the symbol for two-way implication or "if and only if," ↔.)

Let us now take up one of the problems I raised a moment ago: how to deal with complex nouns like *fish that live in the sea*. From now on I am going to use the technical term *common noun (phrase)*, or *CN(P)*, for such items and their simple counterparts, because in common language as well as in much technical linguistic literature the word *noun* covers two types of expressions that are logically quite distinct.) The device that is used in logic and that we will borrow for our analysis of natural language makes essential use of what are called *open formulas*. An *open formula* is a formula that includes somewhere in it a variable that is not under the scope of a logical operator like ∀ or ∃. So, a simple example is one like his: *Run(x)*. A slightly more complicated on is this: *Love(x,c)*. Thus far, such formulas have been defined as *true* or *false* depending on the assignment of values to variables. What we want is some way of turning them into predicates by binding an unbound or free variable. Again, we can introduce the new kind of expression by a new rule for PC and add a corresponding semantic rule to say what it is supposed to mean. Let me say first in words what the new meaning is supposed to be: suppose *x* is the variable that is to be bound by our new operator, then the whole expression is supposed to form a predicate that holds of an individual just in case the formula is true when we consider assignments (otherwise alike) in which *x* is assigned that individual as a value. Here is the new rule:

R8. If *F* is a formula and *x* is a variable, then *LAMBDA x [F]* is a predicate.

S8. *LAMBDA x [F](a)* is true on an assignment *g* iff for all assignments *g'* that differ from *g* at most in their assignment of a value to *x* and such that *g'(x)* is the individual denoted by *a*, *F* is true.

I regret that I have to say that in such a complicated way. Let me give a few examples to clarify my meaning:

8. *LAMBDA x [Run(x)](a)* is true iff the individual denoted by *a*, say Anne, runs.

9. *LAMBDA x [Love(x,b)]* denotes the set of individuals that love the individual denoted by *b*.

As you can see, the meaning of the *LAMBDA* expression in example 8 is just the same as the meaning of the predicate *Run* itself, so here our new operator is not doing much work for us. Example 9 shows how we can use the new operator to form expressions with meanings we could not express before. The next example makes this even more vivid. Because *F* can be any formula at all, even a very complex one, we can form arbitrarily complex predicates:

10. *LAMBDA x [(Fish(x) & Love(x,b))]*: the set of individuals that are fish and love the individual denoted by *b*.

As this example shows, our new operator is very helpful for modelling the meanings of complex common noun phrases in natural languages that use relative clauses and other sorts of modifiers of common nouns, so the denotation of the expression in example 10 comes pretty close to giving us the meaning of an English expression such as example 11:

11. fish that love Bill . . .

(I am using the expression *LAMBDA* here for typographical convenience in place of the usual Greek letter λ. I should also point out that this operator is being used here in only one of its possible ways, for forming expressions that denote sets from open formulas containing the appropriate free variable. More generally, a lambda operator is used to construct names of functions, functions from whatever the type of the variable is to whatever the type is of the expression that is enclosed in brackets. Thus, we can use the same notation to name functions from number to numbers, such as the squaring function or the function that adds 2 to a number to make a new number: *LAMBDA x [x + 2]*. For the time being, we will use the operator only to form set expressions. Notice that I am identifying here, as is usual, a set with a function from individuals that might be in the set to truth-values; that is, what is technically called the *characteristic function* of the set.) Another example of exactly the same kind could be used to model the conjoined predicate italicized in the following example:

12. Mary *walks and talks: LAMBDA x [(Walk(x) & Talk(x))]*.

So something like this binding operator is a good device for symbolizing the logical form of many complex expressions in a natural language like English and was in fact used by Montague in dealing with the two sorts of examples I have given from English: complex common noun phrases with relative clauses, and conjunctions of predicates with *and* and *or*. Let us now turn to the second kind of expression mentioned in the title of today's lecture: noun phrases.

The development of the predicate calculus and its theory of quantification was one of the triumphs of the modern logical tradition in Europe. The names associated most closely with this development are Frege, Whitehead and Russell, and Tarski. This development was part of the development of modern formal logic, in which important parts of logic were given a precise form. Although natural language has always been a source of insights throughout the history of logic, the aim of logic has usually not been the analysis of natural language, but rather the analysis of deduction, especially (in modern times) the kind of deductions common in the mathematical disciplines.

Many of the philosophers and logicians who took part in this development, as I mentioned before, took the view that natural languages were far too obscure, ambiguous, and ill-structured to be amenable to the kind of treatment that they were proposing in their treatment of logic. And some took the view that they were providing something like an instrument for exhibiting what the true logical form for language *should* be, if it were only well behaved. Thus, in a way, their attitude toward language was revisionist. The structure of natural languages, in their view, obscured rather than revealed the logical form that was needed to think carefully about reasoning and argumentation. Nowhere is this attitude more evident than in the famous analysis of definite descriptions provided by Bertrand Russell. Let me take a few minutes to review this account.

The question at issue here is the analysis of sentences such as example 13:

13. The King of France is bald.

I am not concerned with the problem of whether this sentence should be considered false or indeterminate if France has no king, an issue that has been very important in the interpretation of definite descriptions; that is a separate question. Russell supposed that it was to be considered false (I will return to this question in the next lecture). Rather I am concerned with the analysis of the logical form of the noun phrase *the King of France*. According to Russell, sentence (13) makes three claims: one, that there is a king of France; two, that there is only one king of France; three, that he is bald. Let us agree to use *KF* to symbolize the predicate that holds of an individual if and only if the individual is a king of France. Then the logical form of the sentence as proposed by Russell can be displayed in the language PC as example 13:

13. $\exists x \, (KF(x) \, \& \, \forall y \, (KF(y) \rightarrow x = y) \, \& \, Bald \, (x))$.

In words: there is an individual, x, who is a king of France and if any individual is a king of France, then he is identical to x, and x is bald. (Those of you worried about technical details may notice that this formula is not a well-formed formula according to the rules we have had for PC: to make things easier to see I have used the equals sign " = " in its usual way instead of using a two-place predicate *Equal*, and I have used & to connect three formulas instead of two. The former departure can just be considered an abbreviation; the latter is acceptable because we can show that the way we group a series of formulas into pairs as long as they all have the same conjunction (& or v) does not matter.)

Now as you can see by comparing examples 13 and 13', the logical form proposed by Russell bears little resemblance to the form of the English sentence. The most striking difference is that the noun phrase *the King of France* has been pulled apart into several different pieces of the formula. The same thing is true in a slightly less striking way in a sentence we looked at earlier and that we are able to give a fuller symbolization for now:

2. Every child was teasing a tiger.

If we ignore the problem of the tense and aspect for now, we can give one of the readings (corresponding to example 2) as follows:

14. $\forall x \ (child(x)) \rightarrow \exists y \ (Tiger(y) \ \& \ Tease(x,y))$.

That is, for everything it was true that if it was a child then there was something that was a tiger and that it was teasing. Again, there are no units or constituents of the logical formula that correspond to the English noun phrases *every child* and *a tiger*.

Now, if there is one thing that I believe about universals in syntax, it is that all languages, no matter how different their structures, have a type of constituent or category that we call noun phrase, and further I believe that in all languages this category includes not just things like names or pronouns (as in PC) but also expressions such as *three fish, every child*, and *some tiger*. (I do not mean that the internal structure of such noun phrases is constant across languages. That is clearly false.) If the logicians' languages such as PC are supposed to be getting at the heart of the logical structure of language, wouldn't it be strange that natural languages show such a very different way of expressing things such as examples 2 and 13?

In the next part of my lecture, I would like to show you Montague's way of solving this problem in a way that does justice to the actual structure of natural languages and to the undoubted logical differences that exist between simple noun phrases such as *John*, on the one hand, and more complex ones such as *every fish* or *a tiger*, on the other. But first, let me restate the problem from the point of view of the linguist. I have said that in English (and, we might claim, in every language) noun phrases of the simple and complex sort appear in much the same sorts of positions: they can be subjects or objects of verbs, objects of prepositions (I am speaking very "Englishly" now), and so on. *If* we expect some regular relationship between syntactic categories and the types of meanings or denotations that they can have *and if* we take the sort of structure given by the logicians in such logical languages as PC as coming close to giving a picture of the basic logical structures of natural languages, *then* the syntactic generalization I have just made about noun phrases is a surprise, if not a problem. Now, Montague's general theory of language *did* lead him to expect such a regular relationship between syntax and semantics. There is just such a regular relationship between PC and the interpretation we have given it. Recall that Montague's thesis claimed that natural languages could be treated as interpreted formal systems in just the same way as the logical calculi can. One statement to this effect is found in his first paper on natural language, "English as a formal language" (1970: Paper 6 in Montague, 1974):

15. "I reject the contention that an important theoretical difference exists between formal and natural languages."

(To understand the exact import of this rejection, one must understand that Montague is speaking as a philosopher and logician and that the word *theoretical* is to be understood from this point of view and not from the point of view of the empirical linguist, for whom there are undoubtedly many "important theoretical differences" between formal languages such as PC and natural languages such as English and Chinese. I suspect that what Montague meant was more or less what I cited in my first lecture as Montague's thesis.)

The idea that Montague used to solve the problem at hand may be traced back to the philosopher Leibniz. We might paraphrase it like this:

16. Two things are identical iff all their properties are the same.

(Teachers I know often like to use the example of a detective story here: the detective has the idea that there are two different people A and B, of whom he thinks that A is the murderer. As the story goes on the detective discovers that A and B have more and more properties in common, hypothesizing finally that they have *all* properties in common and are hence identical.) Montague's way of adapting this idea was to interpret noun phrases uniformly as sets of properties. To take a simple example first, we can see that the following two ways of talking are equivalent:

17. John is in the set of walkers.

18. The property of being a walker is in the set of properties that John has.

I am glossing over some technical details here, having to do with the difference between properties and sets in Montague's theory. They are not important in the present context (although they will be later), so let me restate what I have said in a way that conforms more to our previous usage. Let me say (temporarily) that noun phrases are interpreted as sets of sets and accordingly restate sentence 18 as sentence 19 (however, I will use the two ways of talking about sets of sets and sets of properties interchangeably today):

19. The set of walkers is a member of the set of sets to which John belongs.

This is a very powerful and fruitful idea. I will address it for the rest of today's lecture and most of the next lecture as well. For now, let us see how Montague used this idea to deal with complex noun phrases like *every child* and *a tiger*.

First, think about what kind of a set of sets we could assign as a denotation to the noun phrase *every child*. Consider two children, Tom and Sam, each with his unique set of properties. They must be unique, if Leibniz's idea (example 16) is right, and Sam and Tom are different children; we can be sure that they will differ at least on the two properties of being identical to Sam and being identical to Tom. Which of their properties do we want to put into the set of properties that we assign to *every child?* It seems clear that we want to put into the latter set just those properties that they have in common and leave out those properties in which they differ. That is, in technical terms, we want to take the properties that are in the *intersection* of the two sets of properties. Suppose we now keep adding one child after another, each time putting into the set that we are constructing just the intersection of the new set with what we have already and leaving out properties that are different. Now, if we take the leap to *all* children, we can see that the right answer to our question is this: the set of properties that we want to associate with the noun phrase *every child* is the *intersection of the property sets of all children*. Or, in other words:

19. The denotation of *every child* is the set of properties that all children have in common.

What is in this set? Well, for one thing, we can be sure that the property of being a child is in it. What else? The answer to that question, I maintain, is not to be sought in linguistics. If all children love to play, then the corresponding property will be in it. So will the property of being a person and so on. But all that we need for building an explicit semantics for English is the *idea* of this set so that we can do justice to the logical structure of English and to the syntactic structure of English.

We are now ready to show how Montague's analysis of noun phrase semantics allows us to treat simple and complex examples in a uniform manner. Consider these two sentences:

21. John talks.
22. Every child talks.

Sentence 21 is interpreted as sentence 21' and sentence 22 as sentence 22':

21'. The property of talking is a member of the set of properties that John has.
22'. The property of talking is a member of the set of properties that every child has.

Let us now consider the interpretation of *a tiger*. Perhaps you can guess the answer already. Given our aim of giving a uniform type of denotation to every noun phrase, we know that the answer is going to be some set of properties. What set? Again, let us start from a very small universe in which there are just two tigers, A and B. Consider this sentence:

23. A tiger is roaring.

For this to be true, it must be true that *some* tiger has the property of roaring. So we can take the two property-sets of A and B and form their sum or *union;* that is, the set of properties that is in one set or the other, or both, and look into this set. And, once again, as we expand our universe to include more tigers, we keep repeating this operation of forming unions. So the denotation of the noun phrase *a tiger* is *the union of the sets of properties of all the tigers that there are.* So if all tigers are striped, then this set will include the property of being striped, but it will also include the property of being a male tiger and the property of being a female tiger and also the property of being identical to A and of being identical to B. We can say the same thing in a way that is a little more literally what Montague said in *PTQ:*

24. The denotation of *a tiger* is the set of properties *P* such that there is some tiger that has property *P*.

Now we can again show how this interpretation allows us to give a completely parallel interpretation to our new noun phrases (compare 21 and 22' above):

25. A tiger talks.

25'. The property of talking is a member of the set of properties that *some* tiger has.

Let us now turn back to the formal language that we have been building on the basis of PC. We want to ask whether we can deal with the new kinds of interpretations that Montague assigned to noun phrases within that formal language. The answer is, "No." The reason why can be seen in sentence 24, where I tried to say clearly in English what the noun-phrase *a tiger* is supposed to denote. You will notice that I helped myself to a little bit of unordinary English to try to make my statement clear and simple. What I mean is the variable *P*. If you think back to my formal description of the predicate calculus language PC, you will remember that we did have variables, but they were strictly variables standing for individuals such as you, me, or this table. In order to have a formal language that will give us a way to represent the kind of interpretation that Montague wanted to give to noun phrases, we need to be able to use variables over sets or properties. This is an essential and important difference between languages like PC (so-called *first-order* languages) and the language used by Montague to translate and ultimately interpret English (a so-called *higher-order* language). If this way of proceeding is right, then we have learned something important about the semantics of natural language, and his discussion raises an important general question we want to keep in mind:

26. What is the expressive power of natural languages?

My inclination as a linguist, and one continually awed by the beauty and power of natural languages, is to expect that the answer to this question is going to be something like this:

27. Natural languages are as expressive as we, their users, want to make them.

But the discussion above gives a hint of how we can approach fairly precise and interesting questions and answers of this sort by using the tools of modern logic and formal semantics.

Montague made free use of such higher-order variables for properties (and even higher-order ones). Besides the two types of complex noun phrases I have illustrated (with *every* and *a*), he also provided an exactly parallel analysis for noun phrases such as *the tiger,* which reproduced Russell's analysis in terms of a set of properties. So, example 13 about the King of France receives this interpretation:

13". The property of being bald is a member of the set of properties that (the unique individual) the King of France has.

If I were conducting a course in Montague grammar, I would now probably take the time to show how we could extend PC to make it possible to express statements about sets of sets or properties. But I want to avoid complicated formalizations here as much as possible so that we can keep our minds on the important ideas without getting distracted by details. (To work out what we have talked about today, all you really need is a set of variables for sets or properties—Montague used *P*s and *Q*s (still treating the two terms *set* and *property* as synonymous, unlike Montague)—and an extension of the use of the operator LAMBDA to bind these new variables. So the set of John's properties, that is, the denotation of *John,* would be symbolized like this (using *j* as a constant denoting John): *LAMBDA P [P(j)].*

For the classical quantifiers (universal and existential) of the predicate calculus, Montague's treatment turns out to be completely equivalent in truth-conditions to the standard formulations (and hence, adopting Russell's analysis, for definite descriptions such as *the King of France*), and so also for the analysis of simple noun phrases such as *John.* Let us take a moment to convince ourselves of this fact. Recall that a sentence such as, "A tiger walks," is true at a world and time just in case there is some individual both in the set denoted by *tiger* and in the set denoted by *walks* at that world and time. The new way of talking is going to say that the same sentence is true (at a world and time) just in case the property of walking is in the union of the sets of properties of all the individuals that are tigers (at that world and time). But this will be true if and only if there is some individual tiger that has a property-set that includes the property of walking (at that world and time). I think that you can see that the two interpretations will have to be true in exactly the same circumstances, that is, worlds and times. Consequently, the two interpretations are *logically equivalent.* (Let me remind you of what we thought about in the first lecture. To say that two formulas or sentences are logically equivalent is to say, in model-theoretic terms, that they are true in just the same models and false in just the same models.)

We have just covered the essentials of Montague's theory of the interpretation of nouns and noun phrases. I would now like to take some time to show you how Montague developed a treatment of English that accounts for the kind of scope ambiguities involving quantifiers that we looked at earlier (the examples about children and tigers).

As a setting for this exposition, let me remind you of the discussion of compositionality from the earlier part of this lecture. Let us sharpen this idea a bit by stating it in the form of a thesis:

28. *Compositionality:* the interpretation of a complex expression is a function of the interpretation of the parts out of which it is composed and the way in which they are combined.

Let me also remind you of our discussion of how to approach the problem of ambiguity in natural languages. I said that most current linguistic theories, including all those associated with or derived from the transformational theories of Noam Chomsky and his coworkers, assume that certain kinds of ambiguity, including the scope ambiguities we want to consider now, are attributed to different *structures* at some level of representation. But there is another way of meeting the compositionality requirement that does not follow this most usual method. The central idea, like so many others in our current theories of logic and semantics, may be attributed to Frege. In more recent times, however, the philosopher Peter Geach (1972) pointed toward a way of thinking about this problem that was adopted and elaborated by Montague in *PTQ*. I will first reproduce a bit of Geach's discussion and then show how Montague elaborated on it.

Geach's basic idea (basing himself both on the classical tradition of the ancient Greeks and work of medieval European philosophers) was the following. Consider sentence 29:

29. John loves Mary.

There are two ways in which we can think of this sentence as being put together at the last stage of a constructive derivation. We can represent these two ways as in examples 29' and 29":

29'. John + _____ loves Mary.
29". John loves _____ + Mary.

Here, the blanks show where the remaining parts of the sentences are to be inserted. In each case, we have a noun phrase plus something else, a sentence that is missing a noun phrase, but in different places. In effect, this second part is an open sentence, interpreted in a certain way. We should now be able to say exactly how we should interpret such an open sentence so as to be able to put it together with a noun phrase denotation (a set of sets or properties) in such a way as to get a proper denotation for the resulting sentence. Evidently, what we want to do is to interpret the sentence with a blank as a property or set, and that is exactly what our operator LAMBDA enables us to do. So, corresponding to the two ways of putting things together to get sentence 29, we will have these two interpretations.:

30. The property of loving Mary is a member of John's property-set (for 29').
31. The property of being loved by John is a member of Mary's property-set (for 29").

Geach emphasized that these two ways of putting together the sentence did not in any way make the claim that there was a *syntactic* difference between them. (The idea that we can associate two meanings with two ways in which we construct the very same object is what I attribute to Frege.) Notice that what we have done conforms to the requirements of the compositionality thesis stated in sentence 28. In each case, we can state precisely what the denotation of the whole is on the basis of the denotation of the parts and the way in which we have put them together. This view we may call the *derivational theory of interpretation* because it is based on the way we derive a structure rather than on properties of the structure itself. The second way, which does insist on different structures for different interpretations, we may call the *configurational theory of interpretation*. The derivational view is sometimes called the *rule-by-rule* hypothesis because it is explicitly stated in Montague's requirement that every syntactic rule have a unique semantic rule associated with it.

Now, in the simple example that we just looked at, the way we derive the sentence is not important. If you think about it, I think you will agree that sentences 30 and 31 will hold or not hold in just the same worlds. But if we turn to more complex noun-phrases, then we can immediately see how the order of the derivation will indeed make a difference and precisely the sort of difference that we were worried about in our discussion of children and tigers. Here are schematic representations of the final steps in two derivations for example 2 available from the setup of Montague's *PTQ:*

(2) Every child was teasing a tiger.
(2'): Every child + ———— was teasing a tiger.
(2"): Every child was teasing ———— + a tiger.

We can paraphrase these two interpretations in English like this:

32. (2'.): The property of teasing a tiger was in every child's property-set.
33. (2".): The property of being teased by every child was in some tiger's property-set.

And again, these two interpretations differ in just the right way to correspond to the ambiguity we discussed earlier. Moreover, we have shown how it is possible to develop a derivational compositional theory to account for the ambiguity that does the same job done by setting different structures in configurational theories of interpretation, including both the type assumed in my 1968 paper (at the deep structure level) as well as the current theories of Chomsky and his associates (where this sort of difference is expressed at a level of representation called *LF* for *logical form*).

Once again, we have covered a great deal here in a relatively short exposition. I have tried to emphasize Montague's basic important ideas without getting lost in technical formal details. We have, in fact, talked about everything that is essential in Montague's theory of the model-theoretic interpretation of English with one big exception. We will put aside this exception for a later lecture, but let me give you just a bit of a preview. Put briefly, we have concerned ourselves only with that part of this theory that is adequate for situations where we are dealing with real children and actual tigers (whether any actually exist). I have laid out Montague's theory of the interpretation of noun-phrases but I have only shown how it works in such so-called *extensional* contexts. To be concrete, we have only enough at our disposal to know how to deal with a sentence such as 34 in the case where there is some specific, existing unicorn that Mary is looking for.

34. Mary is looking for a unicorn.

But this sentence supports a perfectly clear and essentially different interpretation, one in which there is no such unicorn, in fact, in which there never have been any unicorns and never will be any, but Mary still may be truly said to be looking for one. This interpretation raises the question of *intensional* contexts and objects, and I will return to it in the fifth lecture. In the next lecture, we will look again at Montague's interpretation of noun phrases as sets of properties, but in a more general way. We will see that this theory has had surprising and fruitful implications for the study of natural language semantics.

Lecture IV:

GENERALIZED QUANTIFIERS

In the last lecture, I introduced Montague's theory about the interpretation of noun phrases. *Noun phrases* are interpreted in this theory as sets of sets or sets of properties: *John* is interpreted as the set of sets to which John belongs or the set of properties John has. I used these two ways of talking interchangeably. Today I want to put this theory into a larger setting. It will be convenient and clearer for us if we choose the first way of talking and stay with it, so today I will just talk about sets of sets. (Sometimes, writers prefer to say *families* of sets to make clear that they are presupposing a system that avoids the paradoxes that arise when we talk too freely about sets of sets, but I will just say "sets of sets" for the sake of simplicity and uniformity.)

Before we get into the main subject for today, I would like to review some general ideas about sets, relations among sets, and similar concepts. I have slipped in talk about sets and functions at various points in the previous lectures. I think it would be good to stand back a bit and look at these ideas more closely.

The idea of a set and the mathematical theory of sets are both basic to large parts of modern mathematics and logic. In fact, an important program of research started out to provide a foundation for all of mathematics in set theory. The basic notion of set theory is that of *set membership*. We can take this idea and define important relations between sets on the basis of this primitive idea. One set *A* is a *subset* of another set *B* if and only if every member of *A* is also a member of *B*. The *empty set 0* is the set that has no members; the *universal set U* is the set that everything belongs to. (In our model structure, we've been calling this universal set *E*.) The *intersection* of two sets is the set of things that are members of *both* sets; their *union* is the set of things that are members of *either* set (or both). The *complement* of a set is the set of things (in *U*) that are *not* in the set, and so on.

In the first lecture, we used this kind of talk when we were giving an interpretation to predicates in PC, and in the last lecture we also used these ideas to talk about Montague's interpretations of common nouns (sets of things) and noun phrases (sets of sets of things). In the first lecture, when I talked about the interpretation of transitive verbs such as *love* and *see,* I also talked about sets, but this time sets of ordered pairs; I could have gone on to talk about sets of ordered triples for verbs such as *give.* From these discussions, we can see that there is a very close relationship between the kind of structure we come out with when we talk about a formal language such as the predicate calculus and the kind of structure that we have in set theory. For example, just from our explanations of the logical connectives & and v *(and, or)* and what I have just said about intersections and unions of sets, you can see the connection: the intersection of two sets is the set of things that are in the first set *and* in the other set; the union the set of things that are in one set *or* the other. (Think also about *not* and set complementation and about the *if . . . then* relation $(\rightarrow)$ and set inclusion).

I've also freely talked about *functions*. I hope I have used this word consistently in the precise sense the word has in mathematics and logic, at least in the contexts in which this sense was important. Again, this is a very fundamental idea in mathematics and, in my opinion, in linguistic theory as well. So let me take a minute to say exactly what it means. A (single-argument) *function* is a relation between two sets such that for any element in the first set there is (at most) one unique element in the second set that stands in that relation to it. In other words: way: a *function* is a mapping from one set (its *domain*) that gives a unique member of the second set (this set is called its *range* or *codomain*). We talk about functions as taking *arguments* to give *values*. Consequently, given a function and an argument that is in its domain, we get a single value when we apply the function or the mapping to that argument. Mathematicians and logicians like sets and functions, and Montague was no exception. His model structures for interpreting natural and artificial languages are built up out of sets and functions. Putting together what I just said about sets and relations and what I said about functions, a two-place or *binary* relation is just a set of ordered pairs, and a *function* is just a special kind of relation or set or ordered pairs, namely, one in which if you look at two elements with the same first member of the pair, the second one will always be the same. In general, a function can have many different names and can be defined in many different ways. If you are left with the same set of ordered pairs, then, in this mathematical sense, it will always be the very same function. This characteristic of mathematical functions will be very important in our next lecture, and I will remind you of it then. It is the view Montague followed. It has an inherent beauty and cleanness to it, but it is also a potential source of trouble.

These ideas extend to relations among more than two sets. In general, an n-place function is an $n+1$-place relation where for any one ordered n-tuple of elements that make up the first n places, we always get the same last $(n+1$th) element. So, along with one-place functions like the function from shirts to sizes of shirts, we can have two-place functions from pairs of shoes to shoe sizes, or from twins to mothers, and so on. An important fact about many-place functions that Montague used in his analysis of English is this:

1. Given any n-place function where n is two or greater, we can find an equivalent series of one-place functions (to functions) that go step by step to get the same result.

An example of this is given by Montague's analysis of English verbs that correspond to the two-place predicates of our formal language PC. According to 1, we can think of the denotation of *see* not only as a two-place relation between individual (a function from ordered pairs to truth-values) but equivalently as a one-place function from individuals to sets. This way of looking at it corresponds to the linguistically motivated syntactic analysis of English that says example 2 has the analysis of example 3:

2. Mary sees John; and
3. Mary + sees John;

and that the second part of sentence 3 has a further analysis as in sentence 4:

4. sees + John.

Here we can say that *sees* denotes a one-place function from individuals to sets and that *sees John* denotes a set, namely, the set of things that see John. (Some of you may wonder how this explanation can go together with the theory of noun phrase interpretations that we talked about in the last lecture. This is a very good question, and I will return to it at a later point in these lectures.)

After this side journey through some details about sets and functions, let us turn back to our main topic for today; that is, more about the interpretation of noun phrases.

The main motivation that I gave for Montague's interpretation of noun phrases as sets of sets in the last lecture was this: that interpretation allows us to give a uniform syntactic and semantic treatment to simple and complex examples such as *Mary* and *every tiger that Mary saw*. As it happens, even stronger arguments can be found for such a view.

We saw that for the classical quantifiers *every* and *some* as well as for Russell's analysis of definite descriptions with *the* (which is constructed with the help of these quantifiers), we obtained an interpretation that was logically equivalent to the classical analysis in a first-order language like PC. But many quantifiers are found in natural language—both everyday language and the language of science and mathematics—where no such first-order equivalence exists.

To understand this fact, it will be helpful to look again at a natural-language statement and the closest equivalent we can get in PC:

> 5. Some tiger walks.
> 6. $\exists x(Tiger(x) \ \& \ Walk(x))$.

Notice that example 6, literally, does not exactly paraphrase sentence 5. What example 6 really says is:

> 7. Some *thing* is a tiger and walks.

I have italicized *thing* to emphasize that the range of the variable x—the things that can be assigned to x as a value—is just the set E of individuals. To say that in another way: in first-order languages such as PC, we always *quantify over the whole domain of individuals*. This does not work for all noun-phrases in natural language, however, as I will now show you.

Here is an example of a sentence that takes us beyond the capacities of first-order quantification:

> 8. Most fish swim.

It is not just difficult to represent the correct interpretation of a sentence such as example 8 in a first-order language like PC; it is literally impossible. And the problem lies precisely in the fact about PC that we just took note of: in PC, as in all first-order languages, we are always quantifying over the whole domain of individuals. I think you can see the difficulty that we run into if we try to paraphrase example 8 in a way that parallels the way we can paraphrase strictly first-order sentences:

> (7) Some thing is a tiger and walks.

How could we continue example 9?

> 9. Most things are. . . .

Or, to look at it from the point of view of PC, what could we put in for the question mark in example 10?

10. *MOSTx (Fish(x)?Swim(x))*

None of the PC connectives—and we now have *all* the PC connectives—will work. We cannot replace *?* by *&*. That would mean: most things are swimming fish. Nor can we replace it by the implication sign we used to interpret *every*. That would mean: most *things* are such that if they are fish they swim. We can construct a little world where that would be true but where our normal intuitions would say that example 8 is false. Let us say that *most* indicates something similar to "at least two-thirds." Now, consider a world in which 100 fish live, of which only 25 swim. My intuitions tell me that example 8 should be considered false in such a world. How should we interpret *MOSTx F?* Suppose it is true if and only if for at least two-thirds of the relevant assignments of values to variables F is true, on the analogy of our semantic rules for the other quantifiers. On 25 assignments that assign x a thing that is a fish, $(Fish(x) \rightarrow Swim(x))$ will be true; on 75 other assignments to fish, that formula will be false. All we need is to have enough other things that are not fish to assign as denotations of x to outnumber the nonswimming fish and the putative interpretation of the "formula" will be true (note that if $g(x)$ is not a fish, by the laws of logic, the implication will be true). And so on for the other connectives. So, what does sentence 8 really mean? A natural statement of the truth condition for example 8 is something like this:

11. Sentence 8 is true (at t and w) if and only if most of the things that are fish swim (at t and w).

The point here is that in order to judge the truth of example 8, we must look not at the whole domain but at just exactly the subpart of the domain that is comprised of fish in the domain. Sentence 8 says something not about most *things* but about most *fish*. (Facts like these give us an important clue about *why* natural languages have the syntactic category of common nouns. *Common nouns* are expressions that give a natural basis for picking out those subsets of the domain that we want to quantify over in sentences such as sentence 8.)

In his analysis of English in *PTQ,* Montague restricted himself to noun phrases with denotations that *can* be reconstructed through the use of the classical quantifiers of first-order logic; however, his general method of interpreting noun phrases as sets of sets works perfectly for the analysis of noun phrases such as *most fish* and the many other kinds of noun phrases that natural languages use. If we look at the full range of such expressions in natural languages—for example, noun phrases using words and phrases such as *many, few, more than half, at least two*—we quickly see that the classical quantifiers are very special and that most (!) natural language noun phrases of a complex sort are like *most fish* and not like *every tiger* in this respect. In the last several years, a great deal of very fruitful work has been done that takes this more general perspective as a point of departure. I would now like to talk about this work.

As it often happens, this work on natural language turned out to have a connection to work in mathematics and logic that had been developed for completely different reasons. This branch of mathematics is one that I have used for the title of today's lecture: the theory of *generalized quantifiers*. I need to warn you of a source of confusion in the use of the word *quantifier*. In classical logic, a *quantifier* is a thing like ∀ or ∃; that is, a thing that goes together with a variable to bind free variables in a way that we've gone through in our discussion of PC. In the theory of generalized quantifiers, a *quantifier* is something that corresponds to a whole noun phrase meaning of the sort that Montague used and that we look at last time. Here, I will use the term in this latter sense. So the denotations of expressions like *John, every fish, most tigers,* and so on, will be called quantifiers; not the meanings of things such as *every* or *some*.

What is a *quantifier* in this new sense? It is what I have been saying about noun phrase meanings in Montague's theory of English. Let me put this down carefully and explicitly:

12. A *(generalized) quantifier* is a set of sets (included in the domain *E*).

(In the following, I assume we have a specific domain *E* in mind and hence suppress reference to the domain.) Let us get used to this idea by restating some familiar example in this new style:

13. *Mary* denotes the set of sets of which Mary is a member.
14. *a tiger* denotes the set of sets whose intersections with the set of tigers is not empty (is not = 0).
15. *every child* denotes the set of sets that the set of children is included in.

As you can perhaps see from these examples, it is helpful to have some notation for definitions of this kind, because definitions written out in English can become fairly complicated. In line with our general purpose, which is to understand the main ideas and not get bogged down in notation, I will not introduce any such notation here.

(Parenthetically, it is worth noting that sometimes people talk about quantifiers not as meanings but as expressions having those meanings. For clarity, I will use the term *quantifier expression* when I mean something that denotes a quantifier.)

I think that you will be able to see that these definitions are really equivalent to those we have seen already. Let us verify this by thinking about example 15 and comparing it to what I have said about the denotation of *every child*. In the previous lecture, I gave the following definition:

16. (= example 20 in Lecture III) The denotation of *every child* is the set of properties that all children have in common.

I also gave another equivalent formulation: *every child* denotes the intersection of the property-sets of all children. (Remember, the term *set* is used consistently in this lecture instead of *property*.) We can restate this last statement in terms of the intersection of the set of sets to which each child belongs. Example 15 says that a particular set is a member of the denotation of *every child* just in case the set of children is a subset of that set. But to say the latter is to say that a particular set is a member of the quantifier just in case every member of the set of children is a member of the set in question. So the set of walkers will be in the set just in case every member of the set of children is also a member of the set of walkers. Thus, we can give the following three paraphrases of sentence 17's meaning:

17. Every child walks.
    i. If anything is a child, then it walks.
    ii. The set of walkers is a member of the intersection of the sets of sets to which each child belongs.
    iii. The set of children is included in the set of walkers.

These sentences are all equivalent.

What can we say about the interpretation of words like *a, some, the,* and *every?* We call these expressions *determiners*. Given the theory of generalized quantifies, we can define this class of expressions semantically. They are expressions that go together with common nouns (simple or complex) to make quantifier expressions. Remembering that common nouns denote sets, we can say this:

18. A *determiner* is an expression that denotes a function from sets to quantifiers (sets of sets).

Trying to write in English the denotation of a word such as *every* is rather complicated. But you can see what it would be like by substituting a variable over sets (say M) for *child* and *children* in example 15:

19. *every M* denotes the set of sets that the set of Ms is included in.

If we go back one further step, then we can say what *every* means:

> 20. *every* denotes that function f from sets to sets of sets such that for all sets M, $f(M)$ = the set of sets that the set of Ms is included in.

You can see how we would proceed if we went on to give definitions of the denotations of *a (some)*, starting from example 14.

At this point, it is a fair question to ask what all of this complicated machinery is good for. (It *is* complicated.) I will answer this question by giving some examples.

Many linguists have asked the same question about the whole program of Montague semantics and other related model-theoretic approaches to semantics. I think that the only convincing answer to questions of this sort is to demonstrate the way we are able to explain and understand things that we were unable to explain or understand without such a theory. The study of the generalized quantifiers of natural languages has been one of several areas where we have been able to approach explanations of puzzles that have resisted solution in linguistic work that was carried out without an explicit model-theoretic semantics. These new explanations are squarely based on properties of the model-theoretic entities that we use to give accounts of the semantics of natural languages. There is a saying: "By their fruits shall ye know them." It is only by producing results and raising interesting new questions that new theories and approaches can justify their right to be studied. I want to go through a few examples of long-standing problems in English linguistics that linguists have come to understand a little better by using the tools of model-theoretic semantics.

The first problem is posed by sentences that start with the English word *there:*

> 21. There is a pig in the garden.
> 22. There were three sailors standing on the corner.
> 23. There are many solutions to this problem.

(The word *there* is unstressed and is not the same as the location or place word *there;* it corresponds to Chinese *yŏu*. Sentences 21, 22, and 23 sound fine, but there are many sentences we could make up that do not sound so fine:

> 24. ?There's every tiger in the garden.
> 25. ?There were most men in the room.
> 26. ?There are all solutions to this problem.

That is, some restriction seems to be placed on the kinds of noun phrases that can occur comfortably in the position after *there* + *be* in such sentences.

Many linguists have tried to give a good characterization of the property of noun phrases that is at work here but with little success until lately. Most "solutions" amounted to little more than marking the noun phrases with an arbitrary feature (definite/indefinite or the like). This amounts to labelling the problem and not solving it. No obvious syntactic explanation has been found for the judgments that we have about such sentences.

Work on the generalized quantifiers of natural language and the determiners that give them their semantic values has provided a truly semantic solution to this problem. It requires references to a model-theoretic property of determiners that I will now explain.

Remember, *determiners* are interpreted as functions that take sets to form sets of sets. Another way of thinking of the meaning of *predicates* is as functions from objects of some kind to truth-values (as I noted earlier): given an argument, they yield the value *True* if the argument is in the set, *False* if it is not. They are questions, so to speak, that say *Yes* or *No* about the membership of an element in the set that they are characterizing (hence, as I said, they are called *characteristic functions*). Looked at in this way, *quantifiers* are functions from sets to truth-values. For some determiners, however, no matter what set they are given and no matter what world or model is looked at, the set that is given as an argument will *always* be a member of the set of sets that the quantifier expression denotes. And for others, the argument set will *never* be a member of the quantifier, independently of the model or world. In terms of questions, the quantifiers associated with such determiners will always say *Yes* for every set and model, or will always say *No,* as long as they are given a set for which they are defined. Such determiners are called *strong* determiners (*positive* or *negative* strong, according to whether the constant answer is *Yes* or *No.*) All other determiners are called *weak* determiners: they are the ones for which the answer to the question depends on the model. In some models, the answer will be *Yes,* in others *No.* Let me state this property as follows:

27. Consider a determiner *D* and a set-denoting expressions *N* (a common noun phrase) and the statement:

    D N is/are N.

    If the truth of the statement depends on the model, then *D* is *weak.*
    If not, then *D* is *strong* (*positive* or *negative*).

The following are some examples; are the determiners strong or weak?

28. Every tiger is a tiger.
29. All tigers are tigers.
30. No tiger is a tiger.
31. Many tigers are tigers.
32. No tigers are tigers.

33. The tiger is a tiger. (Take *the tiger* here to be about a specific individual tiger and not the kind "tiger.")
34. Both tigers are tigers.
35. Neither tiger is a tiger.

Do not be hasty in your judgments! We need to think very carefully about the definitions of *weak* and *strong* just given, if we use questions about examples like these as tests for the characteristics of particular determiners. To help you better understand the definitions and to reinforce some of the ideas about models I have described rather quickly herein, I will go through some of the examples:

28. *every* is a (positive) strong determiner because sentence 28 must be true for every model. To verify this, we need to think about various models. Suppose there are some tigers in the model. Then sentence 28 must be true because they will all be tigers. Suppose there are no tigers in the model. Thus, in this model, *D*(tiger) is the empty set. But, then, sentence 28 must be true because the empty set is a subset of every set. In fact, anything we say about tigers will be true in this model. In this model, every tiger talks, every tiger speaks English, every tiger is a lion, a pig, a swan, a telephone pole, and so on. (Sometimes we say that such a sentence is "trivially" true in such a situation.) Similar considerations lead us to say that *all* (sentence 29) is a positive strong determiner.

30. *no* is a weak determiner, and a little reflection is needed to see this. Again, think of the same two models, one with, one without tigers. In the first one (with tigers), sentence 30 is false, because to say it is true would be to say that nothing exists that is both a tiger and a tiger. We could also put this in terms of the denotation of the quantifier expression *no tiger*. What set of sets do we want this to be? (I leave this as an exercise.) Consider now the second model (without tigers). This time the sentence is true, so the truth of sentence 30 depends on the particular model that we choose. Hence, *no* is a weak determiner.

33. To understand how the definition 27 applies to sentence 33, we need to see something about the analysis of *the* that has to be presupposed in order for our explanation here to work. Recall Russell's analysis of definite descriptions. According to that analysis, sentence 33 would be true just in case there was a unique tiger in the model and it was a tiger. That is, in models with more than one tiger or no tigers at all, sentence 33 would be false. So, according to Russell's analysis, the truth of the answer would

certainly depend on the model and *the* would be a weak determiner. This situation is one where the proviso I slipped in that the quantifier be *defined* plays an essential role.

One of the important improvements in the analysis of definite descriptions after Russell was the following: Many philosophers — Strawson (1950) was the first, I believe — have argued that the uniqueness part of the analysis should be thought of not as a direct part of the truth conditions for sentences with definite descriptions but rather as a precondition for the appropriate use of such sentences. One reason for this decision is that according to Russell's definition, in the case where there is more than one king of France (or here: tiger), the negation of the sentence would have to be true, and this runs counter to our intuitions. We can reconstruct this idea by saying that a sentence like the one about the King of France (sentence 33) is just undefined as to its truth value when the presupposition of uniqueness and existence fails. We can accomplish this by defining the denotation of the determiner *the* in such a way that it has no value or is undefined when its presupposition of uniqueness and existence is not met. Whenever the presupposition of a sentence using a definite description (that there is a unique King of France or tiger) is met, sentence 33 or a sentence such as sentence 36 will be necessarily true:

36. The King of France is a king of France.

Therefore, *the* is, after all, a (positive) strong determiner. The facts we will now discuss can then be taken as evidence for Strawson's ideas about definite descriptions as opposed to Russell's. (You might wish to go through the other examples; *both* and *neither* are like *the* in being defined only if certain presuppositions are met.)

I now return to the problem of sentences with *there*. If we go through a lot of sentences with *there* and various determiners, we can see that an exact correlation is found: sentences in which the determiner of the noun phrase after *be* is strong sound bad; those where it is weak sound good. Why is this so?

To find an explanation, we must think about the interpretation of *there* sentences. Here is the interpretation Barwise and Cooper (1981) suggest:

A sentence of the form *there be NP* is interpreted as meaning that the set of individuals in the model *(E)* is a member of the quantifier denoted by the NP.

What does this mean? Look at a simple example such as sentence 21:

(21) There's a pig in the garden.

To say that the set of individuals in the model is a member of the set of sets denoted by *a pig in the garden* is to say simply that the set of sets that some pig in the garden is in has the set of things in it; that is, that the intersection of the set of pigs in the garden and the set of things in the model is nonempty. Example 21 will be false just in case no pig in the garden is in the model. Such sentences are truly informative about the model just in case they are neither necessarily true nor necessarily false. But sentences of this form with positive strong determines are necessarily true, those with negative strong determiners necessarily false, independent of the model. So they never tell us anything interesting and hence sound peculiar.

(You may have noticed that this analysis assumes, somewhat controversially, that in a sentence such as sentence 21 the entire remainder of the sentence after *be* is a single constituent noun phrase. It is not clear to me that this assumption is correct. Whether this analysis or a popular alternative in which *a pig* and *in the garden* are separate constituents is correct is an interesting question. If the latter analysis is correct, the task of providing an insightful semantics that will support an equally convincing semantic explanation for the facts discussed is a challenge for future research.)

For a second example of a long-standing problem for which the model-theoretic approach provides new insights, I would like to take up the phenomenon of so-called *negative polarity expressions*. These are items like the italicized ones in the following examples:

37. I did not see *any* lions.
38. *I saw *any* lions.
39. I have not *ever* been to China.
40. *I have *ever* been to China.
41. No student who knows *anything* about phonology would *ever* say that.
42. Every student who knows *anything* about phonology would (**ever*) say that.

Such items have been discussed a great deal in the linguistic literature since the earliest days of generative grammar. The first few examples illustrate why these expressions have been called *negative polarity* items. But even since the earliest days (Klima, 1964), it has been clear that it is not just negative elements that provide the right environment for the proper use of such elements, as the first part of sentence 42 demonstrates. Again, as long as we try to characterize the environment that licenses the use of such polarity items in a purely syntactic way, we are left with an arbitrary marking of items as *plus, minus,* NEG, or the like. Such examples provide a second case where a model-theoretic approach seems to offer a new kind of insight. Once again, I must digress to explain some technical matters.

The semantic properties of determiners and quantifier expressions that are crucial in characterizing the proper use of polarity items have to do with the possible entailments of sentences and the relations between the sets involved in interpreting sentences containing quantifier expressions. Let us adopt a standard picture of a sentence that exhibits the logical structure relevant for the following discussion. This structure follows almost exactly the syntactic form of the sentences involved:

    43. Every fish swims: $D (A)(B)$.

Here, D stands for the determiner *(every)* meaning, A for the set that is the argument of the determiner meaning (corresponding to *Fish*), and B for the set (corresponding to *swims*) that is the argument for the quantifier. We are interested in entailments that hold when we vary A and B under relations of set inclusion.

Suppose we pick a set B' that contains B as a subset—in this example, perhaps the set denoted by the expression *moves*. We now ask whether it follows by pure logic that if sentence 43 is true, then sentence 44 must also be true:

    44. Every fish moves.

Sentence 44 does indeed follow. In such a case, we say that the quantifier denoted by *every fish* is *upward-entailing* and so also by extension the quantifier expression (think of going "up" along the set inclusion relation). That not every quantifier is upward-entailing can be seen from the next example:

    45. No fish walks.
    46. No fish moves.

Sentence 45 may be true and sentence 46 false, so that—assuming the set of walkers is a subset of the set of moving things—the quantifier expression *no fish* is certainly not upward-entailing. In fact, it has the "opposite" property of being *downward-entailing*. If we pick a set that is included in the appropriate set B, then we do get an entailment. So from sentence 46, assuming it were true, we could conclude that sentence 45 would be true, as would sentence 47:

    47. No fish swims.

We can characterize different kinds of determiners in the same way by asking about subsets and supersets of the set A (as in the picture of sentence 43). Assume that animals are a superset of fish and carp a subset of fish. Now consider these sentences:

(43.) Every fish swims.
48. Every carp swims.
49. Every animal swims.
(45.) No fish walks.
50. No carp walks.
51. No animal walks.

Sentence 43 entails 48 but not 49. Sentence 45 entails 50 but not 51. So both *every* and *no* are downward-entailing determiners. (Think of some upward-entailing determiners.)

Now we can say something precise about the characterization of elements that allow the use of polarity items of the sort that we have been discussing.

52. The expressions that license the use of negative polarity items denote downward-entailing functions. The polarity item must be contained in an expression interpreted as the argument of the function.

If we look back at our original examples 37 though 42, we can see that this characterization works out just right. Take sentence 37 for example: if I did not see any lions, then I did not see any male lions, young lions, old lions, and so on. If I have not been to China, then I have not been to Tianjin. Students who know about phonology include students who know about autosegmental phonology and so on.

Once again, interesting open question exists about the details of this account (drawn from Ladusaw, 1979). For example, whether we need to pay attention to purely syntactic relations instead of or along with the purely semantic property of being the argument of a function I have appealed to in 52 is controversial. It is also quite appropriate to notice that although we have provided a promising model-theoretic account of the licensing conditions for polarity items, we have not really given an *explanation* that makes use of the interpretation of the polarity items themselves. This task remains to be done.

I have given two examples where a model-theoretic approach appears to give promising results in helping us understand certain phenomena that we encounter in natural languages. In both cases, it seems as if we can put the weight of explanation on the semantic component of our theories. In this way, we are able to provide a very simple account of the syntax of the construction dealt with: sentences with *there* and sentences with polarity-sensitive items such as *any* and *ever*. Both explanations made essential use of the theory of noun phrase interpretations as generalized quantifiers, a theory for which we found independent arguments of two sorts: first, English noun phrases require such an interpretation if we are to give a uniform semantics for various kinds of noun phrases, both simple ones such as *John* and *Mary* and complex ones such as *every tiger that growls;* second, many, perhaps *most,* determiners of natural languages form noun phrases that simply cannot be paraphrased in the classical quantification theory of first-order languages like PC. Actually, we can look at these last two points in a different way. A theory of the sort we have been presuming makes two assumptions or hypotheses:

I. The semantics of natural language is compositionally linked to the syntax.
II. The logical form for natural language is very close to if not identical with the surface syntax of the language.

The evidence we have found, then, including the two kinds of examples that we look at, may be taken as evidence for the explanatory power of theories that incorporate Hypotheses I and II.

I would now like to look briefly at a different approach to the logical form of English sentences; that is, that of the family of theories associated especially with the recent work of Noam Chomsky and his coworkers, including the approaches that have come to be known as government and binding (GB) theory. I will first say something about some important differences in goals and assumptions of these theories as compared with the theory we have been looking at. Then I will argue that the two kinds of theories are not as incompatible as they are sometimes thought to be, at least with respect to the kinds of issues we are interested in pursuing in these lectures.

The major difference in goals between the two kinds of theories lies in the role and importance of semantics in the sense that we have been assuming here. In GB theory, as well as in related approaches, giving an explicit semantic interpretation to the structures generated, described, or licensed by the theory is not necessary. Thus in GB, we have considered various levels of representation—S-structures, D-structures, LF (Logical form), PF (phono-logical form)—and although semantic judgments, for example about the relative scopes of quantifiers and so on, play an important role in arguing for and against various proposals, no interpretation is given to the structures by any explicit set of rules. Thus, from our point of view, all the levels are purely syntactic levels, linked by various sorts of rules or conditions. Comparing the situation here in the syntax with the situation in phonology is interesting. In recent years, questions of phonetic interpretation have played an increasingly important role in phonology. I consider the lack of interest in semantic interpretation a rather serious defect. It not only makes overall comparisons between model-theoretic approaches and GB difficult, it also makes assessing the evidential value of various judgments about essentially semantic matters, such as "coreference" and scope, difficult.

The important question here is: Is this difference a matter of principle or of choice? I believe it is the latter. One passage in Chomsky's *Lectures on Government and Binding* (1981/2) seems to suggest that one could, if one wished, take the LF structures of GB, or perhaps some further level of "semantic representation," and provide a model-theoretic interpretation for them (Chomsky refers to this interpretation as "real semantics" [p. 324, the quotation marks are his]). I see no reason why this could not be done, and, in fact, several people have actually worked out interpretations along these lines. There is a serious theoretical issue here, however, that concerns the exact nature of the relation between the syntax and the semantics. GB, like related theories in the transformational-generative tradition, has assumed without argument that the relation is to be characterized by a mapping defined on syntactic objects of some kind (D-structures, S-structures, LF-structures). In Montague grammar and many related approaches, as I have indicated briefly, the relation between the syntax and semantics is not of this sort. Rather, a relation exists between syntactic *rules* and semantic *rules*. This constitutes a different and interesting hypothesis, the so-called *rule-by-rule hypothesis*. I will not address this question here, because I am concentrating on the semantic interpretation itself and not on the relation between the syntax and the semantics (however, I will address this question briefly in Lecture VIII).

I now wish to return to a more particular topic, the relationship between the treatment of noun phrases in GB and the interpretation of noun phrases as generalized quantifiers that I have been discussing today. I will show that, on this point, the two theories are compatible. In fact, the generalized quantifier approach gives a very nice semantics for the treatment of noun phrases in GB, and, if we take over one detail from Montague's analysis of intensional verbs such as *seek,* we will actually solve a problem for the GB approach.

First, I must address briefly the GB analyses of quantification. As you may know, scope relations among quantified noun phrases are characterized by the use of a rule of quantifier-raising (QR), which moves a noun phrase from its base-generated place in a structure and adjoins it to a sentence node (we may ignore other possibilities here) leaving behind a trace or empty category. So, details aside, we might derive two different LF-structures from the S-structure for a sentence such as sentence 53:

53. Every child was teasing a tiger.

These two LF-structures correspond to the two kinds of interpretations we considered in the last lecture:

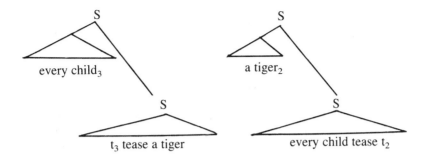

How are we supposed to interpret these structures? It seems as if we can take over directly the kind of interpretation that Montague gave in 1973, both for the noun phrases and for the remainder of the sentence. The noun phrase can be interpreted as the appropriate generalized quantifier—that is, set of sets—in each case, and the remainder of the sentence, with the trace acting as a variable, can be taken as denoting a set. We can use the lambda operator if we wish to give a clear representation for such an interpretation. In fact, the usual informal notation given by Chomsky and others for the quantified noun phrase suggests that the noun phrases should be interpreted as restricted quantifiers: *for all x: x a child*. But such restricted quantifiers are exactly the same as generalized quantifiers.

Let me indicate briefly how Montague's theory might form the basis for an improved theory under GB assumptions. I mentioned toward the end of the last lecture that we had not yet discussed the question of how to interpret a sentence such as example 54 in the case where we do not want to claim the existence of any unicorns.

54. Mary is looking for a unicorn.

We are still not quite ready to talk about the real interpretation for this reading of the sentence, but we can indicate how it is derived in *PTQ*. The interpretations we have discussed thus far have been those where Montague's grammar used a special rule of "quantifying in," a kind of transformation that substitutes a noun phrase for a variable and at the same time changes other occurrences of the variable into pronouns. (This is slightly inaccurate: in sentences with no negation, some of our interpretations could also be derived directly for noun phrases in subject position.) Another way in which noun phrases can occur in sentences in Montague's analysis is that they can be generated in place directly. With an intensional verb like *look for*, this direct generation of object noun phrases provides for an interpretation that does not require the existence of unicorns at all for a sentence such as sentence 54. Now, in GB theories, the apparent obligatoriness of QR for quantified noun phrases has always presented a problem. It is in the spirit of such theories to let all rules be optional. Thus, in a GB analysis, the natural move is to let QR be optional also with no special conditions or filters. The interpretation of a sentence in which QR has not applied can then be taken over directly from Montague's theory.

In this lecture I have given you a brief look at some of the interesting consequences of adopting Montague's theory of noun phrase interpretations. We have seen that this point of view offers elegant solutions to several long-standing problems that have resisted analysis in other approaches. Of course, I have only touched on the possibilities here. In the last several years, extensive work has been conducted on the theory of generalized quantifiers as applied to natural languages.

Lecture V:

KINDS OF THINGS

Before we begin today, let me take a few minutes to do a bit of geography on these lectures. If you are going somewhere on a bus, you often like to know how far you have come and where you are going next. Consequently, I would like to map out the course. In the first three lectures, we were getting accustomed to basic ideas from model-theoretic semantics, in particular, Montague grammar, or better, Montague semantics. I've said very little about Montague grammar as a theory of syntax *and* semantics. (By the way, in contrast to many linguists (see, for example, Dowty *et al.*, 1981) I think that Montague grammar in this latter sense is a very interesting theory and worth exploring as an alternative to many other theories, for example, Chomsky's government and binding theory (GB), or Bresnan's lexical-functional grammar (LFG, see Bresnan, 1982), and I and several other linguists have done a fair amount of work in the last years in such exploration, especially of the categorial grammar that is a basic part of the theory exhibited in Montague's *PTQ* (for some references, see the endnotes to this lecture.) In one week, then, we had a very rapid introduction to the fundamental ideas of Montague's possible world semantics and of model-theoretic semantics. Here are some of the basic things that we covered: the idea of a formal language; the interpretation of a language by a model structure; an interpretation function; and a set of assignments of values to variables forming the basis of standard quantification theory. All of this was by way of getting at the fundamental question of the course: What kinds of model structures are appropriate for interpreting natural languages. We looked first at what is *almost* the simplest model structure for a formal language. (The simplest model structure is the one used for interpreting the so-called *propositional calculus,* where the primitive elements are just unanalyzed formulas or sentences and the structure is just the set $\{0, 1\}$ of truth values.) That was what we called *M1: E,* the domain of individuals, and $\{0, 1\}$, the pair of truth-values. We then looked at a richer model structure, *M2,* which adds to the structure *M2, W,* and *J,* the sets of worlds and times. Then we looked at the way Montague used this apparatus to solve the problem of getting interpretations for complex common noun phrases and for full noun phrases, or term phrases, as they are often called. In our last lecture we started already to go "on beyond Montague," by looking at how his theory of noun phrase interpretations as sets of properties (or sets of sets) was just a special case of the more general and empirically necessary view of noun phrases as generalized quantifiers and we studied some of the interesting results that have come from this view in pointing toward solutions for outstanding puzzles in linguistic analysis. Let me reemphasize that these examples are particularly important as answers to the following quite legitimate challenge to model-theoretic semantics as a valid theory for empirical linguistics: what can you do or explain with these methods that you cannot do or explain without them?

Except for the topic of generalized quantifiers, what we did earlier represents a kind of skeleton recapitulation of the first stage of work in the formal semantics of natural language. During this period, linguists and philosophers were getting to know each other's work, the problems about which they worried, the differing criteria of adequacy they were accustomed to, and so on. But most of the details of Montague's semantics were taken over unchanged. In the last lecture and for the remainder of the lectures, we are looking at some examples of a second phase, which is now going on. In this phase, enough common ground and familiarity with the technical aspects of the theory has been prepared for people to go ahead with proposing various extensions, restrictions, and fundamental changes in the theory, still trying to answer the fundamental question: What model structures are adequate for natural languages? (A second fundamental question is still very much alive, as it has been all along: What is the best sort of relation between syntactic and semantic structures?)

Before continuing, I want to make two things clear: First, our survey has been sketchy in that I have taken Montague semantics as the main example for exploration. Please note that there have been other exemplars, more or less independent of, and more or less similar to Montague's theory. (See endnotes to this lecture.) It is probably fair to say that Montague's theory has been the most influential. Second, many details of interest are found in Montague's work and work done more or less directly under his influence that we have not touched on at all. I will mention some of them as a base from which to start as we take a look at some recent and current developments in semantic theory.

The main topic today is *kinds of things*. Notice that in all our model structures so far we have had just one big domain, E, consisting of all the entities or individuals or things that we can use to interpret our language. I have not said anything about what these things are: they could be concrete objects like you or me or this table, they could be abstract objects like numbers, or the idea of virtue or honor, just anything. Now, when they are introducing interpretations of this sort, logicians usually say something like this: we do not care what your things are, it is no part of logic to decide this question, you just give them to us and we will tell you what you can do with them. I think that is a proper attitude for logicians to take. If we are interested in empirical questions about language or in the philosophy of language, however, it is not so clear that this is an adequate answer. By the way, some philosophers get very worried about talk of properties, or propositions, or possible worlds, and so on, because they think they are very "mysterious entities," but they seem perfectly happy to talk about a fixed and given domain of individuals. The notion of a thing seems pretty mysterious also, however, no less and no more than the notion of a property or a possible world or a proposition.

We can change this simple picture in two ways: one is to introduce more structure into the domain E. The other is to introduce whole new sets of things into the model structure, just as we introduced worlds and times as new primitive elements. Today we are going to concentrate on the first sort of approach; next time on the second. In each case, I will add more detail about Montague's theory as a base and try to show how the puzzles that led to the suggested changes did not seem to have an adequate solution within Montague's setup.

Let me first review and expand a bit on the structure of *M2*, the basic model structure of Montague's *PTQ*. As we've seen, the primitive elements that are used in M2 are distributed into the sets $\{ 0, 1 \}$, E, W, and J. Out of these sets, Montague constructed a hierarchical system of possible denotations by allowing denotations to be functions of almost all kinds that we could build up with these sets as a base. For example, we can have functions of the following sorts:

1. $E \to \{0, 1\}$.
2. $E \to (E \to \{0, 1\}$.
3. $\{0, 1\} \to \{0, 1\}$.
4. $E \to E$.
5. $\{0, 1\} \to E$.

Example 1 represents the set of functions from individuals to truth values and so on for the others. Some of these sets of functions have counterparts (almost) in the interpretation of *PTQ* (examples 1, 2, and 3 do), but some don't (examples 4 and 5 do not). In addition, Montague included as possible denotations, for every kind of entity or function a special additional function from pairs of worlds and times to those entities and functions. These latter sorts of functions are what Montague called *intensions* (with an *s*!). They are what make his logic "intensional." They are also called *senses,* and Montague's theory is a particular example of an attempt to explicate an important distinction that was introduced into the philosophy of language by the German philosopher and logician Gottlob Frege, a distinction between *sense* and *reference.* Many pages have been written about what Frege meant or how we might reconstruct the difference. Very roughly, we might say that the reference is the actual thing (or thing in some world) that corresponds to the expression in question, what it picks out, while the sense is whatever it is that allows us to know how to pick it out, or in more Fregean language: a way of referring to something. (The counterpart term to *intension* is *extension* so that this proportion holds of these pairs of terms: sense: reference:: intension: extension.) This distinction will be of more importance in our next lecture, when we talk about properties, but just to get used to it let us consider two examples of intensional functions in PTQ.

(The reason I had to say "almost" above is this: although all of the above examples of possible functions exist in the general model structure of *PTQ* as possible denotations, not all of them are actually used in interpreting the English fragment directly, nor in the derived interpretations that are used in Montague's stipulations about constraints on admissible interpretations (the so-called *meaning postulates* that I will address briefly in the next lecture). This is partly because of the intensional character of his interpretation we have just considered. For example, the closest counterpart to the functions of type example 3—truth-values to truth-values—is the type for adverbs such as *necessarily* that take *intensions* of truth-values, that is, propositions $(<s, t>)$ to truth-values. The type of example 3 would be appropriate for strictly truth-functional operators like negation, but negation in *PTQ* is introduced syncategorematically (that is, by rule) and no syntactic category exists for words such as the English word *not.* In general, the semantic rules in *PTQ* that correspond to the syntactic rules putting functional categories together with their argument categories or objects apply the denotation of the functional expression—verb, adverb, preposition—to the intension of the denotation of the argument expression.)

Suppose we ask about what corresponds to the meanings of names most closely in *PTQ.* Well, going from our interpretation of PC, we might expect names to correspond to individuals, that is, members of *E,* which is correct, but only partly correct. Even if we overlook the complication introduced by interpreting natural language names as generalized quantifiers, so that $D(j)$ is the set of sets to which John belongs, if j is a constant in our language, certain other kinds of name-like expressions seem to require a different treatment. Consider the expression *Miss America*. Every year in the United States a contest is held in which young, unmarried females compete on the basis of beauty, charm, and talent. The winner of this contest is called *Miss America* for a one-year "reign." Suppose Jane Jones is Miss America this year. In some contexts we can substitute her real name and the pseudonym *Miss America,* and it would not make any difference:

6. Jane Jones is beautiful.
7. Miss America is beautiful.

It seems clear that example 6 can be true if and only if example 7 is true at any world and time. Well, not quite any world and time, because at a different time (namely any time except this year) the two expressions will not refer to the same individual. On the other hand, consider examples 8 and 9:

8. Jane Jones must be beautiful.
9. Miss America must be beautiful.

Here, one can argue that sentence 9 will be true in any world or time, while sentence 8 may be true in this world, but certainly needn't have been true in other worlds. To deal with this difference, Montague introduced two things in his interpretation. The first is the *individual,* which is just what we said it was, namely some member of E. The second is the *individual concept,* which is a function from world-time pairs *to* individuals. Thus, we can distinguish between two ways of understanding the expression *Miss America:* one, the actual person picked out as that individual at a world and time; the other, the intensional function that allows us to find the individual who is Miss America at any world and time. This distinction allows us to understand an ambiguity in a sentence such as example 5:

10. Miss America is getting taller every year.

Gong back to Ms. Jones, sentence 10 could be quite false if we understand *Miss America* extensionally, but quite true if we think intensionally. In his interpretation of English in *PTQ,* Montague based everything on individual concepts, but included a special way of "getting down" to individuals. Later writers, disagreeing with Montague's solution to a certain puzzle that motivated his use of individual concepts, discarded this feature and gave fragments that base everything on individuals (retaining intensional elements for other levels of functions), but arguments remain (such as the one about Miss America) that make me think that it is a good idea to keep the individual concepts around as a possible interpretation (see Janssen, 1984, for a defense of Montague's individual concepts).

The other example of an intensional entity that I will mention very briefly today is the proposition, as Montague interpreted it in *PTQ* and elsewhere. Again following Frege, Montague took the denotation of a formula or sentence to be a truth-value, which is what I have been doing here all along. I said that his theory allowed us to have denotations that were functions from worlds and times to all the kinds of denotations we can build out of truth-values and entities. So also here. A *proposition*, for Montague, is a function from a world-time pair to a truth-value. So the denotation of a sentence like *It is raining in Tianjin* at a certain world and time is just *1* or *0*, depending on whether it is or is not raining in Tianjin at that world and time. But the proposition corresponding to that sentence is a much more powerful kind of thing. It is a function that will tell us for *all* world-time pairs, whether the sentence is true or false. Montague used this idea in saying something about how we should understand words like *believe*, which he took to be relations between individuals and propositions, not sentences or truth-values.

As we can see from these examples and earlier discussions, an infinite number of denotation are found in Montague's semantic theory. They are organized into a hierarchy of so-called *TYPES*. Let me show you how this works. We do it by a so-called *recursive definition*. An example of a recursive definition from number theory is the following definition of the set of nonnegative integers (that is, the whole numbers 0, 1, 2, . . .). Call this set N. We must have one primitive or undefined concept, the idea of the successor or next number. Here is the definition:

    i. 0 is a member of N;
    II. If any number x is a member of N, then the successor of x is also a member of N; and
    iii. Nothing else is a member of N.

Clause (iii), a so-called *exclusion clause,* is necessary to make sure we are creating a definite set that does not include anything besides the nonnegative whole numbers.

Now I'm going to be a little bit technical and introduce some notation that Montague uses in talking about the hierarchy of types. Here is the recursive definition of the set TYPE:

    i. e and t are members of TYPE;
    ii. If a and b are members of TYPE, then so is $<b, a>$;
    iii. If a is a member of TYPE, so is $<s, a>$; and
    iv. Nothing else is a member of TYPE.

Now what are these supposed to mean? We can use these symbols to define the hierarchy of kinds of elements that are in the denotations assigned to expressions:

    a. Denotations of type e are elements of E.
    b. Denotations of type t are elements of $\{\ 0,\ 1\}$.
    c. Denotations of type $<b,\ a>$, where b is not s, are total functions from elements of type b to elements of type a.
    d. Denotations of type $<s,\ a>$ are total functions from pairs of worlds and times to elements of type a.

Let me explain a few words that I have used here. First, definitions like the ones I have just given are called *recursive* definitions, because in all but the first clauses (the "basis") and the last clauses (the exclusion clauses) we find the same things appearing both in the "if" part and in the "then" part. Second, we already know what a function is. What is a *total function?* It is a function where you always get a value for every element in the set on which it is defined. This is an important aspect of Montague's way of doing semantics, and I will return to it later, because it has been called into question in a lot of recent work, where people have argued that we want to have partial functions, functions where you do not always get a value.

    Now we can use this notation to encode what I said a few moments ago about individual concepts (such as Miss America) and propositions. An individual concept is an object of type $<s,\ e>$; a proposition is an object of type $<s,\ t>$. Here are a few more examples to practice:

$$<e,\ t>$$

This is the type of functions from individual concepts to truth-values. Any function from something to truth-values is equivalent to a set, because it tells you for every object in its domain (that is, the set over which it is defined) *Yes (1)* or *No (0)*. This type is what corresponds to various sorts of predicates in Montague's interpretation of English: intransitive verbs such as *walk*, common nouns such as *fish* or *unicorn*. Here is the type that Montague's theory assigns to term phrases (generalized quantifiers):

$$<<s,<<s,e>,t>>,\ t>$$

    Because we can see a t at the very end, we know that we are dealing with a set of somethings. The somethings are properties, that is intensional things of type $<s,<<s,e>,t>>$. What are they? Because of the s at the front, we know that they are functions from world-time pairs to things of type $<<s,e,>t>$. These are sets of things of type $<s,e>$; that is, individual concepts.

    (If you delve into *PTQ,* or read one of the introductory works I listed at the end of Lecture I, you will see that we are skipping a step in Montague's interpretation of a fragment of English. What Montague did in *PTQ* was not interpret "disambiguated English" directly, but rather define another language of intensional logic, IL, give rules for translating English into this language and then give an interpretation for IL. The type hierarchy is built right into the structure of IL. The important thing here is that this hierarchy imposes a certain structure on the denotations assigned—indirectly—to the English expressions given in his grammar. Montague took over the type hierarchy from earlier work by Russell, Church, and others.)

Early extensions of Montague's work often used this hierarchical kind of universe to deal with more kinds of expressions than Montague had included in his fragment. For example, suppose we want to understand sentences such as these:

11. That proposition is false.
12. The fact that it is raining does not bother me.

Apparently, some expressions of English refer to things like propositions and it is natural to think that a noun phrase like *the fact that it is raining* should get the same kind of interpretation as a clause like *that it is raining*. The latter kind of clause was included in *PTQ* and was interpreted as a proposition. Often we find that verbs that take *that*-clauses as objects can also take "propositional" noun phrases as objects:

13. I do not believe that the earth is flat.
14. I do not believe that proposition.

So a natural thing to do (and it was done in Delacruz, 1976) is to let nouns such as *proposition* denote sets of propositions. Thus, they have an entirely different TYPE of denotation. Similarly, if we ask how we are to understand plural common nouns such as *dogs,* that we should think of them as denoting SETS of entities seems natural. We have the apparatus for doing this right in Montague's hierarchy of types. And that is just what Michael Bennett (1974) did in the first serious study of plurals in English within Montague grammar.

But this approach has a problem. To explain this problem, I have to say something abut Montague's theory of the relationship between syntactic categories and the kinds of denotations that go with them. In his theory, part of the interpretation of a formal language is a function that maps syntactic categories into types of denotations. This means that if two words in the formal language belong to the same syntactic category, then they cannot have denotations of different types. Thus, in interpreting English in the way I have just outlined, the common nouns *dog, dogs,* and *proposition,* have to belong to different syntactic categories. This makes me uncomfortable as a linguist, because it makes it a complete accident that the syntax of noun phrases, for example, for these different kinds of common nouns should have anything in common.

Let me stop, for now, with just this hint at why a difficulty arises when using Montague's type theory for getting different kinds of denotations for words that apparently belong to the same syntactic category. For the rest of this lecture, I will explore another sort of approach to the undoubted differences of meaning that words of the same syntactic class seem to exhibit. This second kind of approach takes the position that we can think of E—the domain of individuals—as being structured in some way. I will start with a simple example and then spend the rest of the lecture going into more detail on two topics: plurals and terms for kinds.

Consider the following sentences:

15. Caesar is a prime number.
16. The theory of relativity is shiny.

They are certainly unusual sentences. Most people would say they do not make sense. What are we to say about them? We could say that they are just false. But given our way of looking at meanings, we might want to ask if there could be a possible world in which they were true. My reaction is to say "No." And if I consult my intuitions, I would probably say something like this: the reason that these sentences are unusual is that Caesar (a man) isn't the KIND of thing that can be a prime number and the theory of relativity isn't the SORT of thing that can be shiny (or not shiny).

I am now going to be talking about approaches that quite literally, incorporate such ideas, that is, theories in which the domain E is split into different sorts of things, and we take this difference into account when we build up complex expressions involving words that correspond to different sorts. So the basic structure of our model *(M2)* remains the same, but E is given some internal structure. For the examples just given, we could say that E is the union of two subdomains *E1* and *E2,* say, corresponding to physical objects such as people and cars (which can be shiny) and abstract objects like theories and numbers (which can never be shiny).

Let us think, now, about the meaning of plurals. As you know, English makes an obligatory distinction between singular common nouns *(horse)* and plurals *(horses)*. What are the meaning differences, if any, between these two sorts of expressions? I want to concentrate especially on a particular theory of plurals proposed a few years ago by the German linguist Godehard Link. But I would like to put this question into a slightly larger context, namely that of asking about the relationships between meanings in one language and meanings in another language, particularly with regard to the nature of grammatical or obligatory distinctions and their semantics. This larger question is one that should be raised, but it has not been touched on very much in the tradition of formal semantics that we are mostly dealing with in these lectures. The phenomenon of a required distinction of singular and plural, or singular, dual, and plural is certainly not a universal one. And the question is this: what is the relationship between the meanings of words such as *horse* and *horses* and the meaning of a word like *mǎ* in Chinese, which does not have this obligatory distinction.

This sort of question is extremely important if we are interested in pursuing problems of general linguistic theory in the domain of semantics. In this general line of thought, we are trying to answer the important big question: What is Language? We are also trying to find answers to equally important questions: How do and how can languages differ? These two questions are, in a sense, merely statements of what linguistics is all about.

Some linguists and other thinkers about language seem to take the line that semantics should be or is "more universal" than other parts of linguistic theory. One might want to make this claim for two reasons: One is to say that meanings are determined by thought, the categories of thinking that we all share as humans; the other is to say that meanings are determined by the way the world is, and we all inhabit the same world. There is reason to be skeptical about both of these reasons, and many writers have taken quite opposite views, one in particular which (stated very crudely) says that language is a kind of screen through which we see the world and with which we think. Languages differ in obvious ways. Therefore, we should expect the meanings of words and other expression in different languages to differ quite markedly. While we cannot make *a priori* arguments about these matters, we can propose and test hypotheses about universals of meaning in the same way as is done in phonology or syntax.

To introduce Link's theory of plurals, let me reiterate that Montague's analysis of English dealt only with singulars: singular noun phrases, singular nouns, verbs that go with them (*walks* and not the inflected forms for plurals like *walk, are,* and so on). The denotation Montague assigned to a singular common noun such as *horse,* was just what we did in our interpretation of PC: D(horse) = the set of horses (It differed at the bottom level in the way I indicated earlier in this lecture due to the use of individual concepts.)

I assume you all know what a horse is. What is the denotation of *horses* used as a common noun as in this sentence:

17. These horses are white.

Michael Bennett gave the first answer to this question in Montague-style semantics. Bennett said: *D(horses)* is the set of sets of horses, so that every time we use the word *horses,* we are referring to sets of horses. Suppose we have an individual horse, call him Abraham, then he would fall within the denotation of *horse*. But if we have two horses, Abraham and Bessie, the set consisting of the two of them would fall within the denotation of the plural *horses*.

I am not going to give a lot of arguments against Bennett's idea, but merely present Link's theory as it is—a different way of looking at plurals—because it is a good illustration of "giving more structure to the domain." (One problem with Bennett's theory is this: because the denotations of singulars and plurals is type-theoretically distinct, in the way I outlined before, all of the syntactic categories have to be duplicated, and the predicate *runs* for a singular subject has to be different from the predicate *run* with a plural subject and it is difficult to understand how we can say things such as *Abraham runs and so do those other horses.* I will return to this problem of "syntactic inflation" in the next lecture.)

Link said that every common noun like *horse* has associated with it a certain kind of structure that we get by allowing an operation for forming what he called plural individuals. So we can take Abraham and Bessie and form a plural individual (Abraham + Bessie), which might be the meaning of *Abraham and Bessie* or *those two horses.* And we can then define a certain part-whole relationship such that Abraham is part of the plural individual (Abraham + Bessie). How is this different from Bennett's way? The crucial difference is that these plural individuals are strictly elements in *E,* the domain of individuals. The following illustration shows what such a structure looks like: If we have three horses in the domain, Abraham (A), Bessie (B), and Clara (C), then the substructure of horses in *E* would look like this:

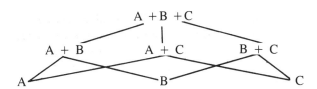

The lines indicate the part-whole relationship I mentioned and " + " (as I used it already) indicates the operation of forming a plural individual—or "fusion"—of two individuals that can continue. Note, however, that the operation is stipulated to be associative—that is, (A + B) + C = A + (B + C)—which is why we are justified in dropping the parentheses and just writing one thing on the top line. The items at the bottom are called *atoms,* they are the things that have no strictly smaller individual parts.

To repeat, Link says the denotations of *horses* is just the set of plural individuals that are horses. Actually, Link did not say that exactly, In order to have a nice algebraic structure, we need to have the atoms at the bottom as part of the substructure in the domain; to give the exact meaning of the English common noun *horses,* however, Link had to exclude the atoms, so the real meaning of *horses* is the set of plural individuals that are horses minus the atoms. And that is something specific about English that has to be said: the denotation of *horse* is just the atoms, that of *horses* just the nonatoms. Every common noun, better, every common count noun in English has associated with it an algebraic structure of this sort. And in English, just as here, we have to exclude the atoms from the denotation of the plural common noun.

Now what might we say about a word such as *mǎ* in Chinese? Suppose we assume that Chinese has basically the same kind of structure associated with each common count noun such as *mǎ*. The we could say that the only difference between Chinese and English in this regard is that for Chinese one does not have to make this special distinction between atoms and nonatoms in the structure. If we are correct, the denotation of *mǎ* is just the union of the denotations of *horse* and *horses*.

$$D(\text{mǎ}) = D(\text{horse}) \cup D(\text{horses})$$

This seems to me to be a rather satisfying way of looking at the difference between Chinese and English in this particular case. And it seems to me that quite a lot of differences between languages with regard to distinctions required in one language but not in another might turn out to be something like this. Notice that there is no sense in which it is claimed that *mǎ* is ambiguous.

I want to be a bit speculative and say something about another striking difference between English (and many other languages), on the one hand, and Chinese (and many other languages), on the other hand: the way in which we count. One of the first things that an English speaker has to learn about Chinese (Japanese, Thai, and so on) is that one cannot merely take a number and a common noun and put them together as we do in English (*three horses, five tables, six pigs*). You have to learn a whole system of *classifiers* or *counters* and put together the right kind of counter and the number word to get the equivalent expressions. So, for example, the classifier for *horse* in Chinese is *pǐ*. Now here's the speculation: perhaps the lack of an obligatory singular-plural distinction and the use of classifiers of this sort go together and might be explained in the following way. Referring to our diagram of the algebraic structure associated with *mǎ* or *horse* and *horses,* we might ask: How many *mǎ* are there? It depends on how you count! If we allow plural individuals that overlap to count as different horses, then there are seven; if we exclude these, then we get a number of possible answers: one (A + B + C), or three (just the atoms), or two (in three different ways: A and B + C; or B and A + C; or C and A + B)—All of which can be very confusing! Suppose the meaning of the classifier is a way of introducing explicitly the difference between the denotations of the singular and plural in English, that is, it restricts the denotation of the common noun to just the atoms: then we have a clear, unambiguous answer. If this is right, then a distinction built into the obligatory distinction in English, gets built back into Chinese, where it counts.

Link's paper treats another extremely interesting topic, the semantics of mass nouns like *mud, blood,* and so on. Briefly, his method is to introduce some more structure into the domain. There is a special subset of atoms in the domain that I will call S (for "stuff"; Link calls it D); the elements of this subdomain are to be thought of as "quantities of matter" and they participate in their own algebraic structure, with their own part-whole relation. Unlike the algebra of count nouns, however, the algebra of stuff is not atomic; that is, there are not necessarily any smallest chunks of matter. (Admittedly, this is confusing because I said they are atoms, but that is within the general other algebraic structure for E as a whole.) Moreover, this domain of stuff is related to the big domain E in a special way: there is a mapping from E to S that preserves part-whole relation in such a way that the stuff corresponding to the individual parts of a fusion of individuals in E must comprise parts of the stuff corresponding to the whole fusion. In English, mass nouns act more or less like all nouns in Chinese: you cannot count them directly. Again, this raises interesting cross-linguistic questions about semantics.

For the remainder of this lecture, I will consider another use or meaning for English words such as *horses,* when used as full noun phrases, as in sentence 18.

18. Horses are mammals.

I will refer especially to Greg Carlson, whose work on such *generic plurals,* as we may call them, was one of the earliest studies within the Montague tradition that suggested a fundamental change in the model structure, again one in which the domain E is given more structure.

At first glance, a term phrase like *horses* seems to be ambiguous. Look at the following sentences:

19. Horses have tails.
20. Horses were galloping across the plain.

In sentences 18 and 19, we seem to be thinking about all horses:

21. All horses are mammals.
22. All horses have tails.

But in example 20 it seems as if we are talking about just some horses:

23. Some horses were galloping across the plain.

For this reason, many people have assumed that there is some kind of a hidden or "0" determiner in a noun phrase such as *horses*. But if we think about it, this seems problematical. First of all, there is what has been called the Port Royal puzzle (because it was discussed in the famous seventeenth-century work, *Logic or the Art of Thinking,* by Antoine Arnauld of the School of Port Royal). Arnauld asked what it meant to say something like example 19 or the following:

> 24. Dutchmen make good sailors.

It does not mean *all Dutchmen,* because we would not count the sentence as false if we found a certain Dutchman who was a terrible sailor. Carlson gives nice examples like this one:

> 25. Chickens lay eggs.

It is certainly false that all chickens lay eggs; only grown-up hens do. The most clinching argument against the idea that ANY determiner is found in the bare plural term phrase is the failure of such phrases to show any scope ambiguities of the sort that we noted in Lecture II with *some* and *every*. Compare these two sentences:

> 26. Some horse eats every kind of fodder.
> 27. Horses eat every kind of fodder.

Sentence 26 is ambiguous with regard to scope of the quantifiers; sentence 27 is not. In this respect, bare plurals act like names, which also do not show scope ambiguities. In short, Carlson's theory treats the denotations of bare plurals in exactly the way in which ordinary proper names are treated. But what are they names of? Once again, we want to think about different kinds of things. According to Carlson's theory, the domain *E* contains three different sorts of individuals: *kinds, objects,* and *stages.* Some sentences with the phrase *horses* are saying something about the individual kind *horse.* Others are saying something about individual instances of the kind. How do we account for the apparent ambiguity in the examples we have just been looking at? According to Carlson's theory, the ambiguity resides in other parts of the sentence. One argument for the conclusion that no ambiguity is found in the bare plural itself comes from sentences like this one:

> 28. Marcia hates rabbits, because they ruined her garden last spring.

Here, in the first clause, *rabbits* is understood generically, but the anaphoric *they* is used in a clause that says something about individual instances.

What is a *stage?* A *stage* is supposed to be something like a temporally/spatially limited "manifestation" of an object or kind. Let me paraphrase two sentences to illustrate the difference:

29. John smokes.
30. John is smoking.

Both sentence say something about the object-type individual John. But the second one says something like this: John is such that there is a stage of him that is smoking.

So to summarize in a much too brief way, Carlson's revision posits this kind of a sorted domain:

$E = O(\text{bjects}) \cup K(\text{inds}) \cup S(\text{tages})$

In addition, two "realization") relations hold across these domains: $R1$ relates both Kinds and Objects to Stages, $R2$ relates Kinds to Objects.

Carlson's work contains much interesting material, and it has formed a starting point for lots of other work (some of which I will address in the next lecture). To end this discussion, I want to share with you an interesting puzzle from ancient Chinese philosophy. (I am indebted to Bao Zhi Ming for this example.) It has to do with the following sentence:

21. White horses are not horses.

Is this necessarily false? If we are thinking simply in terms of sets of things—white horses are things that are both horses and white—then the answer would seem to be *Yes*. But given a theory in which *white horses* involves (as a generalized quantifier) a certain Kind, a genuine philosophical (or scientific) question must be asked: What is the relation between two Kinds with different but related names: *white horses* and *horses*. Notice that, in general, we cannot assume that phrases of the form Adjective + Noun denote sets of things that come under the intersection of the denotations of the two words (fake books are not books).

We have looked very briefly at two developments in which something is done to the model structure by way of introducing different kinds of things, or *sorts* as they are called in technical jargon. Let me end by pointing out a consequence of using sorted domains. What are we to say about sentences in which a predicate that is appropriate to one sort of thing is applied to a term of the wrong sort? One common move is to do something about the truth-value of the model structure, for example, to have three truth-values. Another, not necessarily distinct from the other, is to use not total functions, but partial ones. But that's a long story. I hope we can come back to it in our final session.

Lecture VI:

PROPERTIES AND
RELATED MATTERS

In the previous lecture I talked about kinds and plurals and saw how several linguists had begun to modify the model structure inherited from Montague's *PTQ*. Today, we will continue to look at modifications that have been proposed in the last several years. I also talked about two kinds of intensional objects in Montague's interpretation of a fragment of English, individual concepts and propositions. I will start today by looking at a third kind of intensional element in *M2*, namely, properties.

Recall that, in general, intensional things are all functions of a certain sort, functions from world-time pairs to something or other: individuals in the case of individual concepts; truth-values in the case of propositions. In Montague's theory, properties are functions from world-time pairs to sets. (Because it is not particularly relevant today, I will ignore the time versus world distinction and just talk about worlds.) Consequently, the property of being human is much more than just the set of humans, it is a much more powerful idea, because if I have it, I can travel to any world I want, so to speak, and find the humans in it, if any.

This notion gives us a good start toward understanding certain puzzles that we get into if we think just in terms of sets as the only possible denotations for predicates, as in the standard interpretation of PC (our *M1*).

Here is an example: suppose humans are the only two-legged rational animals. (I say *suppose,* for the sake of the argument; I have my doubts about the rational part.) Take a certain world containing A, B, and C and say they are humans (not horses, anymore) and they are two-legged and they are rational and no other individuals in the domain *E* satisfy these descriptions. Because, by hypothesis, the two common noun phrases *human* and *two-legged rational animal* denote the set { A, B, C}, we should be able to substitute one expression for the other in a truth-preserving way. This is fine for some sentences:

1. A is a human.
2. A is a two-legged rational animal.

But for others, it does not.

3. Necessarily, A is a human.
4. Necessarily, A is a two-legged, rational animal.

Remembering what *necessarily* means, sentences 3 and 4 seem to commit us to the claim that in every possible world humans are all and only the two-legged rational animals, which does not seem right. Or, take the notorious case of belief-contexts. How are we to make sense out of a sentence like this one:

5. Harry believes that A is a human, but he doesn't believe that A is a two-legged, rational animal.

With Montague's theory, we have a start toward understanding these puzzles. It is easy to imagine worlds in which the sets of humans and two-legged, rational animals are different, so the properties in question can be different.

Is this account good enough? I will now present some arguments that it is not.

The difficulty we will discuss is a special case of a much more general problem that arises in model structures of the sort used by Montague that make essential use of a strictly mathematical understanding of functions. In this conception, a (one-place) function just IS a set of ordered pairs (or more generally for *n*-place functions, a set of ordered $n + 1$-tuples). Now, take any necessarily equivalent intensional objects; that is, that give you the same objects for all possible worlds. In this way of looking at things, what we might think should be different intensional objects or senses turn out, after all, to be identical. Let us look at the three kinds of intensions that we have considered thus far.

First, propositions. In this view, all necessary truths express the same proposition, as do all necessarily false propositions. We get into the same puzzle about beliefs that we saw when we took an extensional view of predicates as denoting sets. It seems as if we can make sense out of sentences like this one:

6. Harry believes that $2 + 2 = 4$, but he doesn't believe that $7 + 7 = 14$.

But on this theory, going up to the level of propositions does not help because $2 + 2 = 4$ and $7 + 7 = 14$ express exactly the same proposition. On this view, there is exactly one necessarily true proposition and exactly one necessarily false proposition, and that doesn't seem to be enough.

Next, consider individual concepts. We find similar puzzles about the use of names in belief-contexts. Suppose *the Morning Star* and *the Evening Star* both refer to the same planet (Venus); consider the two sentences:

7. Sally believes that the Morning Star is the Evening Star.
8. Sally believes that the Morning Star is the Morning Star.

It seems as if sentence 7 could be false and sentence 8 true. Here, we might appeal to the difference between sense and reference (as Frege did) to understand the puzzle, but what about necessarily identical things like $5 + 7$ and 12?

9. Sally believes that $5 + 7 = 12$.
10. Sally believes that $12 = 12$.

(Much has been written about these sorts of problems, which I cannot begin to address here. Some suggestions for further reading can be found in the endnotes to this lecture.)

Third, properties. Are there properties in Montague's sense that in every possible world pick out the same sets? A plausible pair is the property of being sold and the property of being bought (this example and the following argument are due to Gennaro Chierchia). Saying that in every possible world in which buying and selling occurs the set of things that are bought and the set of things that are sold must be identical seems reasonable. But now we are faced with a problem. Suppose we want to give a compositional semantics for passive verb phrases with agentive terms such as these:

11. . . . be kissed by Bill.

It seems linguistically well motivated to say that these are built by adding the agent phrase to the passive verb phrase:

12. be kissed + by Bill.

But now we have a genuine problem, on Montague's account of properties, because the following two sentences would have to have the same truth value in all possible worlds:

13. This book was bought by Mary.
14. This book was sold by Mary.

And this is clearly absurd.

For this and a host of other reasons, Chierchia was led to posit a model structure in which properties are primitive entities on a par with individuals and in which genuinely different properties can still be extensionally identical across possible worlds. Before discussing the new model structure that Chierchia has explored, I want to discuss a quite different sort of problem he was trying to cope with. It is related to some of the things that I talked about in my last lecture. And it will help us to see just what sort of creatures the properties are that we might want to put into our new model structures.

Consider these sentences:

15. John is crazy.
16. Being crazy is crazy.

Here it looks on the face of it as if we are saying the same thing about John and the property of being crazy. But on Montague's theory of properties we could not be, because properties and individual concepts are different types of things, so the predicates we apply to them have to be different. Note further that sentence 16 looks like it is attributing a certain property to that very same property, and this is one of the things that the highly hierarchical type theory that Montague used was specifically designed to preclude, in order to avoid the paradoxes that arise in unconstrained set theory.

Let me take a few minutes to explain what the problem is that arises when we try to apply properties to themselves. The problem is a variant of the paradox that Russell discovered in unconstrained versions of set theory where you think that you can talk sensibly about things like the set of all sets that do not contain themselves as a member. Does this set contain itself as a member? If it does, then it does not, and if it does not then it does! The version of this paradox involving properties runs like this: properties have properties, so we can imagine the property *(non-self-attribution)* that a property has when it cannot be predicated of itself: being a unicorn does not have the property of being a unicorn, for example. Now, does the property of non-self-attribution have itself as one of its properties? Same bind: if it does, it does not, and if it does not, it does!

As stated earlier, the kind of typed universe of Montague's model structures (and the corresponding intensional language IL) was developed by philosophers and logicians precisely in order to make it impossible to get into such paradoxical binds. But the use of such strongly typed systems for the semantics of natural languages carries with it a very high price. One part of this high price is the inflation of syntactic categories that we looked at briefly in the last lecture. Another price is that we seem to be unable to model the semantics of many sentences in natural language. For example, think of what the following sentence means:

17. Sally likes everything.

What does *everything* refer to in this sentence? Our intuitions tell us that if example 17 is true we ought to be able to conclude that Sally likes not only cabbages, kings, flying pigs, Joe Jones, and other "ordinary" things, but also the property of being clever, the fact that the earth is round, the smallest prime number, the set of perfect numbers, and so on. Well, using Montague's semantics, we cannot mean by example 17 what we would have to mean in order to be able to draw these conclusions. What to do?

In the last lecture we saw how it was possible to get around a similar problem about plurals by admitting a new kind or *sort* of entity into the domain E of individuals. We can do the same thing here, by simply saying that the individuals in E can include a special sort called *properties:* the property of being crazy, the property of being fun, the property of being a dog, and so on. These new kinds of individuals differ in a crucial way from the kinds of individuals I have talked about so far: they have an intimate relationship to predicates that is not so directly shared by other kinds of individuals. So a natural language expression like *walk* or *love* leads a kind of double life. On the one hand, it can figure in direct predications in sentences such as *John walks* or *Bill loves dogs;* on the other, it can be used in expressions that refer directly to properties such as *Walking is fun* or *To love is to exalt.*

Several difficult technical problems are found when we work out systems that will allow all this to be done; for example, the possibility of paradoxes is still lurking in the background and needs to be dealt with somehow. I am not going to address these problems here (see the endnotes for some references). I will just assert that these problems can be solved and show you what Chierchia's model structures generally look like. (I say *model structures* because several options can be taken and they are being explored right now. I'll lump them all together under the name *M3.*) In *M3,* three kinds of things (besides worlds are found): individuals *(E),* predicates (of varying numbers of places), and everything else. Furthermore, E is sorted into two basic kinds of things: ordinary things and the individual correlates of the predicates (the properties that correspond to them). In addition, we must assume some kind of a function that will give us the individual correlate for each predicate that we can construct. (I am ignoring the kind of further structure we would have if we incorporate something similar to Link's theory of plurals into the model here.)

One nice feature of the sort of setup Chierchia uses is that it can be constructed in such a way as to leave it completely open whether to identify properties that correspond to necessarily equivalent predicates. If one does not, then a straightforward solution to the passive problem (and others like it) illustrated before in examples 11 through 14 is given. Another is that the problem of syntactic inflation does not arise, and we are able to make the kind of sense we want to make about saying that Sally likes everything.

As the examples we have been considering suggest, the topic of properties is intimately tied up with the problem of giving a good semantics for various kinds of nominalizations. Chierchia has also shown how his property theory can easily and elegantly be extended to the nominalizations of adjectives and to an improved treatment of the semantics of bare plural noun phrases, the kind terms that we discussed in the last lectures, as well as to mass terms, as in these examples:

18. This book is red.
19. Red is a popular color.
20. Those horses are dappled.
21. Horses are mammals.
22. This piece of metal is gold.
23. Gold is expensive.

In each of these pairs of sentences, we see first the use of a word in a predicative sense and then a use of the word as a full noun phrase. Chierchia argues that the use of the words as full noun phrases essentially involves their individual property correlates, so that the examples are quite parallel to sentences with verbs:

24. John runs.
25. To run is fun.

What is different are the details of how the nominalizations work in English for the various types of words: adjectives, count nouns, mass nouns, and verbs. I believe that we can begin to see here the glimmerings of a substantive and crosslinguistic theory about the syntax *and* semantics of grammatical categories.

I would now like to turn to another set of topics, which, at first, do not seem to have anything to do with what I have been talking about. In fact, we will see later that they do have something to do with the question of properties and how to model them in our semantic theory. The topic is that of *verbal aspect* or *Aktionsarten* as we sometimes call it, borrowing a technical term from German.

As you may know, one of the hardest things to learn about English is the proper use of the progressive form of the verb (BE + ing). Look at the following sentences:

26. Mary was running.
27. John was building a cabin.
28. Sally was finding a unicorn.

In these sentences, all three of which involve nonstative verbs, the progressive sounds fine, although problems sometimes occur in interpretation and example 28 is slightly funny. But when we try to use the progressive with a stative verb, the results are either very peculiar or demand some kind of special interpretations:

29. ?Bill is knowing the answer.
30. ?Jennifer is believing that the earth is flat.
31. *I am being in Tianjin.

The last one seems downright impossible, hence I have marked it with an asterisk. The other two seem not quite so bad, and we can begin to imagine special circumstances in which we might even use them or sentences that are very close to them.

On the other hand, if we put all of the sentences into the simple present tense, things seem to turn precisely around.

26'. Mary runs.
27'. John builds a cabin.
28'. Sally finds a unicorn.
29'. Bill knows the answer.
30'. Jennifer believes that the earth is flat.
31'. I am in Tianjin.

Now it is the last three that seem perfectly ordinary, and we have to do something special with the first three. Sentence 26', for example, might be used to say something about Mary's habits, or all three might be used as titles of chapters in a book, or as vivid descriptions in "sportscaster style").

This contrast is part of what leads us to distinguish between two kinds of sentences (or other types of expressions), usually couched in terms of the verb involved, although we will see that things are considerably more complicated than that: examples 26 through 28 involve *nonstatives;* examples 29 through 31 involve *statives.*

If we look back at the sentences 26 though 28 and ask about the conditions in which they might be considered to be true, we can motivate a further distinction between the nonstatives. Suppose Mary is running for an hour. Then we might say that during that hour (or at sufficiently many intervals within that hour) the sentence *Mary runs* is true. But if we look at examples 27 and 28, we notice two things. First, it is odd to put these locutions together with adverbials referring to duration of time:

32. ?John built a cabin for an hour/year.
33. ?Sally found a unicorn for an hour.

In the first case we *can* put the sentence into the progressive, but not in the second:

34. John was building a cabin for a year.
35. ?Sally was finding a unicorn for an hour.

And second, even if we can make sense of these locutions, we would certainly *not* be tempted—as we were with example 26—to say that the simple form of the sentence would be true within the interval in question. If John was building a cabin for a year, then it would seem if anything to be *false* that he built a cabin within that year, at least not THAT cabin!

These and a number of other factors lead us to distinguish within nonstative sentences between sentences about *events* such as building cabins and finding unicorns and sentences about processes such as running. To summarize, we have three kinds of states of affairs or happenings:

STATES   PROCESSES   EVENTS

We can, if we wish make a further subdivision of events into those that seem to be instantaneous or momentary and those that take time or are protracted. (This classification has a long history, going back to Aristotle and discussed in more recent times by Ryle, Kenny, Vendler, Verkuyl, Dowty, among many others, see the endnotes to this lecture for literature.) I call all of these kinds of things *eventualities*.

I began talking about statives and nonstatives, which sounds as if we are talking about characteristics of linguistic expressions and have now slipped into talking about processes, events, and states, which sound more like words about things or happenings in the world. And indeed, one of the first things to ask about the distinctions I've just illustrated is this: are we dealing with syntactic (or grammatical) distinctions or semantic ones? The distinctions feel like distinctions in meaning, and although they clearly have some reflections in the grammar of this or that language, I will discuss here primarily the meanings of these various ways of talking about the world. This choice, is, then, reflected in the choice of terms such as event, process, and state.

Consider briefly a few other differences among events, processes, and states. Look at these examples:

36. It took Sally an hour to find a unicorn.
37. Sally found a unicorn in an hour.
38. John built a cabin in a year.
39. It took John a year to build a cabin.

Event sentences are comfortable with frames such as *it took x long to . . .,* or *. . . in an hour/in a year.* Compare the following examples about processes:

40. It took Mary an hour to run.
41. Mary ran in an hour.

Here, we have to do some special interpretation, for example, we have to think about *run* as meaning *run for some preset period* or *begin to run.* Similarly, we have to make up special meanings when we put sentences about states into either of these frames:

42. It took Sam a year to be in New York (meaning, *come to be in New York*).
43. Mary knew the answer in a minute (meaning, *got to know the answer*).

These observations help to motivate the distinction between events on the one hand and states and processes on the other.

Another difference shows up when we try to use adverbials referring to *frequency* or *number of times:*

44. Sally found a unicorn three times.
45. John frequently built a cabin.

Compare:

46. Mary ran three times.
47. Harry frequently believed that the world was flat.

Here, there is nothing wrong with the last examples, but we have to add or understand a little extra (interpreting example 46 as being about events of running, examples 47 about different occasions or periods during which Harry had peculiar beliefs).

Let me mention one final difference that—along with the progressive facts we started from—shows a difference between events and processes on the one hand and states on the other. We have trouble interpreting English sentences in which stative locutions are embedded as complements of verbs such as *try* or *persuade:*

48. I persuaded Mary to build a cabin.
49. ?I persuaded Mary to know the answer.
50. John tried to run.
51. ?John tried to believe that the earth was flat.

Consequently, substantial evidence is found—and I have only mentioned some of it—that we need to make these distinctions in our theories about English (and other languages). The question is: how?

Before suggesting a possible answer, I want to elaborate on Greg Carlson's theory of kinds as meanings of bare plurals in English with which we began to become acquainted in the previous lecture and to connect it to Chierchia's theory of properties.

Recall that Carlson posited three sorts of entities in his domain *E:* Kinds, Objects, and Stages. In addition, he posited two relations of *realization—R1,* connecting Kinds to Objects, and *R2,* connecting both Kinds and Objects to Stages. So we have the following picture:

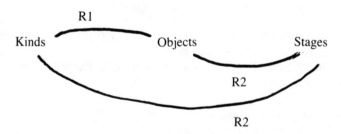

Think about some examples to make the intuitive content of this system a bit more concrete:

52. Fido is running around in the garden.
53. Fido hates cats.
54. Dogs are running around in the garden.
55. Dogs hate cats.

Carlson's interpretations of example 52 and 54 both involve the realization relation *R2* in an essential way. Sentence 52 says that stages of Fido running around in the garden are found, sentence 54 that there are stages of the Kind *dogs* doing the same thing. Examples 53 and 55, on the other hand, are direct predications about the Object *Fido* and the Kind *dog*. What role does the other realization relation *R1* play? It is used to ensure that when sentence 54 is true, there are actual Objects which are instances of (related by *R1* to) the Kind *dogs* involved in the running. How do we ensure they are dogs? Another part of his system requires that any individual that instantiates (that is, realizes according to *R1*) the Kind *dogs* is actually a dog.

Carlson's initial work was done within a more or less standard Montague semantics, the only difference being the introduction of more structure into the domain *E,* as I explained in the last lecture. Within the constraints of this model structure, good arguments were found for rejecting various possibilities of identifying kinds with any of various type-theoretically definable entities of the system, in particular, properties. In Chierchia's model structure, however, the objections raised by Carlson disappear and the way is clear to identifying Carlson's kinds with properties in the new sense. So a noun phrase such as *dogs* can be interpreted as a generalized quantifier based on the individual property correlate associated with the denotation of the common noun *dog,* as I have already indicated, and we have a nicely parallel way of treating various sorts of nominalizations (see examples 18 through 25 and the surrounding discussion above).

What about the realization relations of Carlson in this new approach? Take first *R1,* the relation that holds between *Kinds* and the *Objects* that instantiate them. Quite generally, we need to have something like this relation in our model structure in order to get the right intuitive content for the function mapping predicates to their individual correlates. That is, we want to ensure that a sentence such as the following is true:

56. Fido has the property of being a dog iff Fido is a dog.

We can think of the first clause in sentence 56 as having a denotation that literally models the form of the English expression: English *have* in a sentence like this denotes a relation between an individual and a property. What relation? Well, whatever it is, it seems as if we would want it to follow that sentences such as example 56 will turn out to be true. So we want to say that an entity has or instantiates a property just in case it falls within the extension of the predicate corresponding to that property. Note that this does not commit us to extensionality. There can be two predicates that will be coextensive in all possible worlds, and it will follow from what I have just said that whenever an entity falls within the extension of one, it will instantiate both the property corresponding to that predicate and the property corresponding to the other, but the two properties still need not be identical. In effect, this setup gives us Carlson's first relation *R1* as a basic part of the theory.

Now what about *R2*, the relation between Objects and Kinds and their Stages? Again following Chierchia, we may identify this relation with the relation between things and the stuff that constitute them in Link's system that we studied in the last lecture. Therefore, stages are just the quantities of matter that correspond to individuals at particular times and worlds. This part of the whole system requires more discussion, but I will postpone it to the next lecture. For now, I just want to take this sketch and turn back to the discussion of properties. Given his adaptation of Carlson's theory to Chierchia's model structure we are led to have certain expectations, as indicated in the following chart:

Carlson:	Kinds	Objects	Stages
Link:		Things	Stuff
Chierchia:	Properties	Things	Stuff
Examples:	Dogs	Fido (say)	dog-stages
	Mud	?	(some) mud
	Red	?	?
	Running	?	?
	?	Fido	Fido-stages

The question marks serve to indicate places where we might ask what sorts of entities if any we might expect to complete the pattern. (Link does not discuss the question of what nonpredicative uses of mass nouns and plurals might mean, hence the blank in that row.)

Now I think we are ready to get back to our discussion of *eventualities:* events, processes, and states. The simplest and most straightforward thing to do about accommodating these entities into our model structures is just to "put them in" as elements of the domain, so let us do that provisionally. But the setup we have been exploring allows us to a little more than that, to actually say something about them, and in doing so we will be able to fill in some of the question-marked spaces in the chart above. I want to hold off on a more detailed discussion of this step also until the next lecture, because we need to have one more piece of the puzzle before we can start putting it together into a *big picture*. But for now, just note what we have in our model structure: predicates of various places ("arities"); a big domain *E* with lots of different kinds of things in it; individual property correlates of a number of different sorts corresponding to various types of predicates (common count nouns, mass nouns, adjectives, verbs); "ordinary" things, both singular and plural, like horses, dogs, teapots, and numbers; quantities of "stuff" corresponding to some of the previously mentioned things; and now something or others that are going to be our "eventualities."

Before ending this lecture, I want to say something about a feature of theories such as Montague's that I have yet to mention explicitly, but that has been implicit in some of the discussion we have just gone through: so-called *meaning postulates* (Montague used them but did not use this name for them). A *meaning postulate* is a way of putting some explicit constraint on the models or worlds which we want to admit as possible interpretations of some language, a constraint above and beyond what is built right into the basic model structure that we are using. We were implicitly appealing to some such mechanism a few minutes ago when we were considering what we wanted to say about the relationship between properties or kinds and the things that instantiate them.

Let me first illustrate by way of a meaning postulate that Montague actually uses in *PTQ*. The discussion will also serve to introduce a topic that is of great philosophical and linguistic importance, the interpretation of proper names, a topic that will also be very relevant to our next session.

Basically, two important theories are found about what proper names mean, names such as *Tianjin, John Smith,* or *Crazy Horse*. One is that they are something like disguised or abbreviatory definite descriptions "the *x* such that . . .' "). The other theory denies this and says that names have in a sense no meaning except as ways of referring directly to things. There have been many attempts to make this later idea precise. One of the most famous ones was worked out by Saul Kripke, and it is the one which Montague espoused in PTQ and incorporated by means of a meaning postulate. In a possible worlds framework, real proper names will pick out the very same individual in every possible world, they are hence called *rigid designators* (I suppose a "flexible" *designator* would be something that could pick out different things in different possible worlds). The first of Montague's meaning postulates or constraints on admissible models says as much about the four names in the fragment: *John, Mary, Bill,* and *ninety* (actually it says that about the constants of his intensional logic that correspond to these names): there is an individual who is necessarily (meaning, in every possible world) identical to John, and so on for the others. (Notice that this statement presupposes that the very same individual can appear in many different possible worlds, again a philosophically interesting point of debate. As I mentioned in Lecture II, others, notably David Lewis, deny this and go instead with theories in which different worlds each have their own set of citizens and it is necessary to talk about "counterparts" of these individuals when you move from world to world.)

Other meaning postulates in *PTQ* deal with a variety of matters. Extensionality requirements have the effect of saying that if a certain higher-order intensional relationship holds, then a corresponding extensional relation is found for certain English words. For example, if you see a unicorn, then there is necessarily a unicorn that you see (but if you seek a unicorn no such inference can be drawn). The subject position is guaranteed to be extensional in this sense for all verbs in the fragment (an interesting and debatable point if we extend the fragment to all of English). Another deals with relationships between the meanings of English expressions: *seek* and *try to find*. The interesting point about this last example is that it shows how a theory with an explicit semantics can capture in the semantics relationships among sentences that might be thought to be syntactic in other frameworks.

The important point for us here is that meaning postulates offer a second way to explore the question: what are the most appropriate model structures for natural languages? They allow us to say things about the models of a more fine-grained nature than the "big" things that we say when we set up the general model structures. In our next lecture we'll see that such constraints give us an important clue about the meanings of certain kinds of English sentences and this clue is important for our continuing discussion of kinds of eventualities. For now, let us just notice that meaning postulates can be used to ensure requirements we might want to place on the meanings of various expressions denoting properties, kinds, and the like, of the sort discussed today.

Today's discussions highlight a very serious question (again touched on briefly in Lecture II): What exactly are we claiming when we put forward our theories about model structures for natural languages? The enterprise looks very close to metaphysics or ontology, describing what some philosophers like to call "the ultimate furniture of the world." Do things such as properties, kinds, quantities of pure matter, stages, and so on really exist? I would claim that those are philosophical or scientific questions, not linguistic ones. As a linguist, I feel perfectly justified in sidestepping such questions. Consequently, I like to say that what I am doing here is not metaphysics *per se* but *natural language metaphysics*. Some philosophers claim that all metaphysical enterprise is the analysis of language (this was a prominent part of the program of logical positivists like Rudolf Carnap). But here, too, as a linguist I can be—indeed, I think I *should* be—perfectly neutral. What we are doing is simply seeking linguistic evidence for the nature of the semantic structures that we seem to need to give a good account for the meanings of natural language expressions. Of course, this evidence is relevant to nonlinguistic questions within broader scientific or philosophical contexts. One such context is that of psychology: How do the tentative answers that we find in the linguistic domain relate to questions and answers in other domains such as nonlinguistic cognition, perception, and so on? The broadest such context is philosophical: What is the world really like? how do we fit into it? How do linguistic categories relate to reality? It seems to me that the best contribution that the linguist can make to these ultimate questions seems to be to work out precise theories for linguistic systems as such. I believe that our subdivisions of the world and our efforts to understand it result ultimately from the fact that you cannot say or understand everything all at once. Ultimately, I suppose, this means that we have to remember that our theories will always and necessarily be partial in some sense, because everything impinges on everything, and there will always be a tension between realizing this ultimate limitation and going ahead and chipping away at the mountain with our own small and special tools. Ideas like these are familiar in the great Eastern philosophies and religions. They are becoming more and more part of our Western consciousness as well.

Lecture VII:

SITUATIONS AND OTHER SMALLER WORLDS

A world is a pretty big thing, in fact, as usually understood in possible world semantics, it is everything. Remember our original characterization: a possible world is a way in which things—all things—could be or might have been. Today we will explore some kinds of things that are like worlds to a greater or lesser extent (depending on the particular theories concerned). They all share the property of being smaller than worlds, as normally understood.

Let me introduce this general topic by reflecting on the meaning of the following sentences:

1. The tiger is asleep.
2. Every place has a plate and a pair of chopsticks.

We have already considered a couple of theories about the meaning of *the*. One was Russell's in which the uniqueness and existence part of the meaning of the definite article was actually part of the truth conditions of sentences in which it occurs. We saw in a later lecture that perhaps it would be better to separate that side of the meaning as a kind of presupposition or precondition for appropriate use of such sentences. Either way, in a sentence such as example 1, there must be only one tiger in the world for the sentence to be true. Now, we all know that we do not use language that way. If my wife and I just had a child or even if we had several children and one of them is a baby and I come home from work or she comes home from work and one of us says "Is the baby asleep?," neither one of us believes that there is only one baby in the world. It is the baby that is relevant not to the entire world, but to our particular situation that we mean. Consequently, returning to example 1, in normal situations we would use a sentence such as that when the speaker and the hearer both know that some contextually relevant unique tiger is under consideration. Similarly for sentence 2. Suppose we are having a dinner party and I am serving Chinese food. I ask one of my children to check the dining room table and he comes back and says every place has a plate and a pair of chopsticks, then what does that mean? Remember, in our interpretation, that means every place in the world. Even if we think of *place* as having a particular restrictive meaning, not what *place* means in general but, say, a place at a table which has a chair in front of it, my son surely does not mean every such place in the world has a plate and a pair of chopsticks at it. He is only talking about a restricted situation relevant to our particular conversation at that time. What I am pointing up here is simply that the notion of the world as it is usually taken in possible world semantics is a very big thing, in fact, it is everything. It is all the things that there are and all the relationships they enter into, whether they are here or in the United States or on some other planet or wherever. It is everything about the world, the universe; everything that exists at a particular time. To take that literally as a model and to be always talking about the entire world, the entire way things could be, is at least exhausting! And our discussion of the ways we normally use sentences such as examples 1 and 2 shows that it might be nice to be able to restrict our attention to much smaller models or "worlds," perhaps something like subworlds of the big things that we call *worlds*.

For many years, linguists and others have been talking about discourse situations, contexts of use, and so on. This has been very important work. However, only in the last several years have notions of this sort been coming in to formal work in the model-theoretic line and a number of different people have been thinking about things that are like worlds but are smaller.

I am going to use the term *situation* for these smaller things. We want to be able to talk about a certain situation within a larger situation within a larger situation and so on, and it is only when we get to the largest situation of all that we talk about the whole world in the sense of possible world semantics. A warning: the term *situation* has been incorporated into a certain theory—so-called *situation semantics*—as a technical term. In this theory, as the name implies, the notion of a situation is very important and very basic. Generally, I will use the word *situation* in a nontechnical sense similar to its everyday use. (We will talk briefly about situation semantics in a little bit.)

I will concentrate today on two sorts of theories. The first sort retains the general structure of model-theoretic semantics that we have been looking at: we have a language and a model structure and an interpretation function or relation standing between one and the other. What is different is the structure of the model, in particular, the introduction of situations and relations among them, where the situations are either worlds or something like worlds. In the second sort of theory, there is a new level of interpretation that gets interposed between the language and the model, so we interpret sentences via this intermediate type of object. Along the way, as I take up these theories, I will resume discussion of the problem that we left hanging in the last lecture: the explanation of "eventualities," events, processes, and states.

I have suggested that using "smaller worlds" is a feature of much recent model-theoretic work. The first theory we will look at is actually rather old, dating from a time shortly after Montague first presented his work on natural language to the general linguistic public. It is the theory of Max Cresswell set forth in his 1973 book *Logics and Languages*. In this work, Cresswell is not content to just take the notion of a possible world as an unanalyzed primitive but offers a "metaphysics" of possible worlds, meaning a way of constructing them out of more basic entities. These more basic entities are called *basic particular situations,* and he gives them the name B. The basic particular situations are not themselves analyzed, although Cresswell offers a way to think about them: you could take them to be sets of (occupied) space-time points. This is a very physicalist way of looking at the world, and we are in no way committed to this interpretation (nor is Cresswell). Rather it is a way of keeping things concrete just to help us think clearly about our model structure.

Now what is a world in Cresswell's theory? A world is just a set of basic particular situations in *B*. So the set of worlds is just the set of subsets of *B*, what we call the *power set* of B (which we can write as *P(B)*). This theory gives a definite structure relating various worlds, namely the structure of the power set of a set. This sort of structure is the classical example of what is called a *Boolean algebra*. What is this structure? We have a basic set, as well as the universal set and the empty set, plus the relation of set inclusion, and the operations of forming unions, intersections, and complements. In a Boolean algebra, we abstract away from the particular notions related to sets here and just think of the general structure of elements, relations among them, and operations on them. Consequently, when you run into references to Boolean algebras you can always safely think of the structure of power sets and you will not go wrong. (The algebraic way of thinking has been pervasive recently. In fact, we have run into it already in our discussion of Godehard Link's theory about plurals and mass nouns. Link works with structures that are not Boolean algebras, in general, but share a lot of structure with Boolean algebras.)

Notice that some of these worlds can be very small. Hence, they offer us a way to think about "situations" (in the nontechnical sense) as something like partial worlds. Take the situation of me talking to you in this room. That's a possible world (in Cresswell's theory). But obviously bigger and smaller situations to which this situation or world is related exist as well. One bigger one is the situation of Tianjin during a certain time. One smaller one is the situation (set of occupied space-time points, say) that comprises the area including me and my table and the first row of chairs (over a certain period of time) but not the whole room. We can even think about "worlds" that correspond to individuals such as Joe Jones: say the "space-time world" that he makes up during his life or some limited part of it. Very flexible, this notion of a world in Cresswell's metaphysics. The last example strongly suggests Carlson's notion of stages and Link's notion of quantities of matter or "stuff." Shortly, I will try to follow out these resemblances. Cresswell actually discusses examples of this sort, that is, "worlds" that correspond to various individuals. He calls them *manifestations* of the individuals involved, and we must ask what he means by an individual in this model structure. Cresswellian *individuals* are functions from worlds to subworlds of the worlds that are their arguments. They thus seem to be something like individual concepts in Montague's theory (functions from indices—that is, world-time pairs—to individuals). Cresswell also has *individual concepts,* which are one step up in the hierarchy of functions: they are functions from worlds to individuals (in his sense).

Now I want to say a bit about contexts, because they will be important at several points for today's discussion. Thus far I have talked as if we interpret linguistic expressions simply with reference to a world (and time, in *PTQ*) and an assignment of values to variables. Earlier, however, we noticed that this is not sufficient in the general case. Many expressions in natural language require knowledge about the circumstances in which they are uttered or made in order to make sense of them. Examples are *I, you, here, now,* as well as tenses, worlds such as *yesterday,* and so on. We can hone our appreciation for this fact by examining the following sentence:

3. I am here now.

If we try to evaluate this sentence with respect to a world and time only, then we would have to say that the sentence is always going to be true, which is wrong, as we can see by looking at sentences involving modality:

4. If I were not here now, I would probably be in Massachusetts.

To make sense of sentence 4, which certainly seems reasonable and may even be true, we have to concede that sentence 3 might not be true. This apparent problem is immediately solved if the theory is elaborated. What we have to do is consider first the circumstances in which example 3 is evaluated. This will give us values for the context-dependent parts of the sentence: *I* has got to refer to the speaker, *here* to the place where the sentence is used, and so on. Then, once these context-dependent values are supplied, we can run the sentence through our familiar evaluation procedure. We call context-dependent items like *I, you,* and so on, *indexicals.* We call theories or parts of theories that have to do with the circumstances of use *pragmatic* theories (unfortunately, "pragmatics" is used in a number of different ways, this is only one of them, albeit an important and basic one). Following Montague, I will call the circumstances under which a sentence is uttered, used, evaluated, etc. the *context of use* (sometimes I'll just say *context* for short). (Notice that we must be careful here, hence all the *etc.*'s. Generally, we are thinking about utterances of expressions, but we have to allow for other kinds of "performances." For example, if I read a note written to me by my great-grandfather 100 years ago, to be opened on my fiftieth birthday, what is the context of use?) In general, we have to think of our evaluation of linguistic expressions as going through something like the following process:

Utterance, etc.   *Pragmatics*   *Semantic Evaluation*

Expression   →   Context of Use   →   World, Time, Etc.

To continue, how might we model contexts in our formal theories of meaning? The first idea, propounded by Montague, David Lewis, and others, is to think of contexts as simply *n*-tuples of specifications or parameters: one for the speaker, one for the addressee, one for the time, one for the world, and so on. Notice that on this view, worlds, times, and so on enter the picture two different ways: once as part of the context, once again as part of the semantic evaluation. (You can think of the assignment of values to variables as a context in the setup of *PTQ*.) Now the problem here is with the "and so on." This view makes it seem as if we can set up some prior fixed list of parameters for the context. Again it was Cresswell (1973, again!) who showed that this is an unreasonable expectation: In general, we do not know in advance what elements of the context we will need to get on with the semantic evaluation of a sentence. Cresswell gives a nice example to illustrate this point. Consider this request:

5. Please bring me another quart.

Do we need to have a "previous drinks parameter" to interpret such a sentence?!

Now one thing to notice is this: even though we do not know in advance what elements of the context are required to begin the evaluation of a sentence, any given sentence (or other expression) will always supply just the right questions that need to be answered by the context of use. And this is exactly the same situation that we face in giving the semantic evaluation for any given expression. In the latter case we just *assume* an open-ended thing like a world (open-ended as far as *we* are concerned) that will give us all the information we need for the semantic evaluation. So we can adopt the same strategy here. We can think of the context of uses as a situation, a specially designated situation, which is sitting there with whatever information we need to kick off the semantic evaluation of the expression in question. And in Cresswell's theory, this situation will just be a world. (I should stress that this is *not* Cresswell's theory of contexts as set forth in his 1973 book.)

With regard to Chierchia's theory, what happens when we embed it into a Cresswell model structure? Recall that Chierchia's model structure has a very simple structure: there are just individuals and n-place predicates (propositional functions), and everything else. (I have not said what the last part comprises—It consists of all higher-order functions that are left over, so to speak; they have a very different status in the theory.) Moreover, the individuals are divided into two large groups: those that are the individual correlates of the predicates and "ordinary" individuals. The former can be further subdivided (as we started to do in the last lecture) for meanings that correspond to various sorts of nominalizations: verbal and sentential expressions, kind terms, mass-terms, and adjectives. Now from Cresswell's point of view this is all quite all right, as he says that the elements in the domain can be anything you wish, and explicitly provides for putting higher-order elements back into the domain. (You can look at work like Chierchia's as spelling out a way of doing this very thing.)

If we adopt Cresswell's characterization of individuals as functions from worlds to subworlds of those worlds, then we are allowing ourselves to let Chierchia's property correlates be the same kind of things: so just as John Smith gives us for every world the manifestation of John Smith in that world so the property of Kissing gives us all the events of kissing in that world. And if we identify the properties with the Cresswellian individuals-as-functions we return to the same problem. What to do?

Here, I think we can very well borrow a wrinkle from Link. Recall that Link's model includes a function from things to the stuff that comprises them. This is not to say that the things *are* functions. Indeed, Link was very careful to set things up in such a way that he could separate different things that might be "materially identical," in order to cope with puzzles like the one illustrated in the following sentence:

6. Terry's ring is very new, but the gold that makes it up is very old.

The point here is that two things—the ring and the gold that constitutes it— are mapped (let's say) into the very same quantity of stuff but still have contradictory properties. So instead of saying that individuals are functions, let us say that there is a function—call it EXT—that allows us to find the manifestations of the individuals in the worlds we give them as arguments. So given a world w and an individual i we have EXT$(i)(w)$ as the subworld of w that is i's manifestation in w. And I will identify these manifestations both with the states of Greg Carlson's theory and the quantities of stuff or matter in Link's theory. (It is important not to confuse our EXT function with something found in Chierchia, namely a function that brings you from a property individual to its corresponding propositional function.)

Now, with respect to individual (undifferentiated) we have this setup:

INDIVIDUALS   EXT(INDIVIDUALS)   MANIFESTATIONS

Individuals are just elements of the domain E, the function EXT gives us for each a function from worlds to manifestations (subworlds). Let us now take up the sorts of individuals in turn, by way of a few examples.

JOHN SMITH is an example of what most people (and theorists) think of as an ordinary individual. His manifestations are subworlds of the worlds to which we apply the function EXT(John Smith). We take these manifestations to correspond to Carlson's stages (time-world slices of John Smith) and to Link's quantities of matter or stuff. We can exploit this difference between an individual and its manifestations to get a sortal distinction among predicates that might be applied to the individual. Some predicates seem to relate to the individual as such: John Smith may be intelligent, a linguist, he might know Chinese, and so on. Others seem to relate more directly to his manifestations in some more or less limited world: he might be drunk, speaking English, angry, and so on. (These distinctions seem to get at what people sometimes call essential and accidental or permanent and temporary attributes.) Unlike the next example, we might want to treat his name as a rigid designator in some fashion. (How, in this theory?)

MR. AMERICA, another ordinary individual, but one with very different properties from John Smith, as we can tell by looking at his manifestations. John Smith's manifestations in various (non-science-fiction) worlds have a comfortable continuity. Mr. America's jump all over the place. Moreover, they are organized in such a fashion that we can correlate each chunk of the discontinuous manifestations that we find in any given world with manifestations of individuals like John Smith, Paul Newman, and so on. Definitely not a rigid designator in any sense.

HORSES. Here we have an individual correlate of a propositional function (one-place). As Carlson has argued at length, in English, bare-plural noun phrases such as *horses* share a lot of properties with proper names. Again (as with John Smith above), we get a contrast of predicates that go with the kind as an individual and those that go with particular manifestations of the kind:

7. Horses are mammals, like to run, eat oats, etc.
8. Horses are running in the meadow.

A special relation is found between the property corresponding to bare-plural uses of the English word *horses* and the (ordinary) individuals that fall within the extension of the denotation of the common noun *horse*. This relation is the one that Carlson included as one of his realization relations: the relation between a Kind (now Property) and individual instances of the Kind. Now this is the sort of regular realization that is captured by saying that *horses* is the nominalization of *horse* in English, and a minimal semantics for nominalizations will ensure that this realization or instantiation relationship holds, as we saw in the last lecture. Moreover, each of the individuals that is a horse will be identified with the kind of thing that can have a name, that is, some kind of ordinary individual. Of course, with the last observation we begin to enter the realm of anthropology. What kinds of things will have names will vary a great deal from culture to culture: we give names to individual hurricanes and typhoons, for instance. (Interesting sidelight: we also have common nouns like *typhoon* and *hurricane*—many other names for particular weather conditions in English and other languages—that are rooted in particular individual parts of the world—that is, Planet Earth. Notice that this is not akin to using a proper name for a kind of thing, as in "He is a real Napoleon.")

Taking what we have so far, a typical set of interrelationships might make the following kind of story: There is a horse Abraham. If we follow the theory of names as rigid designators for individuals like Abraham, he is a world-independent individual. Abraham's manifestation at any world (that is, the value of EXT(Abraham) at that world) will be a subworld of that world. These manifestations will be the stages of Abraham (according to Carlson) or the quantities of stuff corresponding to Abraham (according to Link). Abraham is a horse in those worlds where he is a horse. This horse is an instantiation of the Property named by the English nominalization *horses*. As an individual, Abraham has various attributes: he is intelligent, can run fast, etc. Moreover, the property of being a horse (meaning Kind) has various attributes: they can run fast, are intelligent, are mammals, bear their young live, usually one at a time, etc. We have certain expectations about Abraham because he is an instance of a horse: that he will be intelligent, able to run fast, etc. (*Not* that he will bear any young at all, etc.). An even looser relationship is found between the attributes of Abraham as an individual and the attributes we may expect to find for any particular manifestation of him in some smaller or larger world. For example, in any situation in which he is hobbled, we do not expect him to actually run fast. In fact, at certain of his stages (very "late" ones in which he is old and has been put out to pasture) we do not even expect him to run fast if he is unhobbled. Suppose, for example, that a contest for Mr. Horse is held every year that determines another individual. One year Abraham is Mr. Horse. During this year, Mr. Horse's manifestations coincide with Abraham's. And so on. This illustrates that a large part of our actual understanding of things depends on our knowledge (about horses, evidence for attributes of kind and individuals). We want our semantic theories just to give us the general structure of meanings, not the specific content.

MUD. The property Mud is another individual in our model structure. Like Horses it is correlated with a predicate, this time a mass-term predicate. Our setup allows us to find the manifestations of mud in any world: that is, the 'scattered individuals' making up all the quantities of mud in the various situations or worlds. Some writers (Quine, for example) have identified such 'scattered individuals' as the primary meanings of words like mud used as noun phrases in sentences like this one:

9. Mud is muddy.

(Undoubtedly a true sentence.) This view carries with it all the problems of purely extensional interpretations of predicates that led us to abandon PC and its model structure *M1* as a plausible theory about natural language semantics. In the model structure we are exploring here, *mud* names an individual, albeit a different kind from examples such as John Smith or horses. How is it different? It is different from *horse* in a crucial way. The algebraic structure that we associate with words like *horse* and *horses* (as a common noun) is *atomic*. That means that if we look at the horses in any world we will find at the bottom of the structure elements that are the smallest elements that still qualify as horses. Not so with mud. Here we must be very careful in what we say: we are NOT saying that there are not smallest mud-elements—there may or may not be—what we are saying is that this question is left open. We simply do not require as we do with horses that there be such smallest elements or atoms. In general, this seems to be the best strategy: we want to leave things open where language leaves them open. The question about the ultimately atomic or nonatomic nature of mud—or gold or hydrogen—is a matter of physics, not linguistics. With count nouns like *horse,* on the other hand, it does look like natural languages, do force an answer.

RUNNING AND KISSING. Here are two more individuals in our onto-logical zoo, the properties of running and kissing. These individuals, like Horses but unlike John Smith, are the individual correlates of predicates or propositional functions. Like other individuals, we can apply our extension function EXT to them and get function from worlds to subworlds. The values for each world will be all the particular instances of running and kissing in that world, considered as the "stuff" of running and kissing. We can notice an important difference between these two examples, which seems to parallel quite exactly the difference between mass nouns like *mud* and count nouns like *horse*. The parallels and difference can be brought out in these examples:

10. There was a lot of mud in the stable.

11. ?There were lots of muds in the stable.
12. There was a lot of running during the parade.
13. ?There were lots of runnings during the parade.
14. ?There was a lot of horse in the stable.
15. There were lots of horses in the stable.
16. There was a lot of kissing during the parade.
17. There were lots of kissings during the parade.

I use question marks here to indicate the fact that the sentences so marked require us to stretch the normal or unmarked meanings of the main nouns in them. In sentence 11 for example, we have to give some kind of a count meaning to muds—perhaps kinds of mud or blobs of mud; in sentence 14, we have to interpret horse as a mass noun; while in sentence 13 we have to think of individual instances or acts of running. In general, in areas of meaning such as this, speakers of a language have special resources for reinterpreting words in a way to make sense out of somewhat unusual uses. Some languages, on the other hand, have built in ways to express such differences by grammatical means. (The two ways of moving between mass and count meanings for nouns have been called the Universal Grinder and the Universal Packager. Notice that *run* and *kiss* are typical examples of the distinction studied in the last lecture between *process* and *event* verbal expressions and their correlated "eventualities." (I have not marked sentence 16 with a question mark because the Universal Grinder seems to work much more smoothly and unexceptionally in English for verbal expressions than for nominal ones.) We can catch these parallels in a neat way by adapting Link's analysis of mass, count, and plural nouns to verbal expressions. Kissing is atomic, running is not, and we can identify the manifestations of such properties in our Cresswellian version of Chierchia's theory as "quantities of process," the stuff of happenings in the world.

It seems to me that this is a useful framework for thinking about some of the different kinds of meanings that natural language expressions have. Many questions remain, of course, which I have neither the space nor the time to address here. A few examples: what about the meanings of more or less abstract words? We have been considering concrete things such as horses, mud, running, kissing, and so on. They all seem fairly easy to understand in physical terms, as occupied space-time points if you wish. But what about things such as the number 90, or the quality of mercy, or the color green? Tomes have been written about what numbers really are: classes of real objects, things we can construct in set theory, denizens of some ideal platonic realm? Similarly for qualities or virtues like mercy, love, honor. And colors? They do not seem to have any existence apart from our perception of them—I do not mean that we cannot give an account of their physical basis, only that the identification of a certain fuzzy-edged range of light-waves as instantiating the property green does not seem to make much sense apart from the sentient beings that so identify it. These are all interesting questions to pursue. I will address some of them in the next lecture, when we turn to thinking about some other views of semantics and their possible connections to our model-theoretic way of talking about meaning. Right now, however, I want to address another matter that bears more immediately on what I have been talking about today.

Here we are, then, with individuals such as John Smith and Abraham the Horse and others such as Mud and Horses and Running and Kissing. We have noted some sorts of interconnections among them, but many others can be found. In particular, it does not seem as if we will have done an adequate job until we somehow manage to draw some connections between things such as John Smith or Abraham and things such as Running and Kissing. What we need are some "hooks." The hooks that we will explore a bit are provided for us by an aspect of linguistic meaning that has a respectable history in informal approaches to language meaning but until recently has had few reflexes in model-theoretic approaches.

The aspect of linguistic meaning that I am referring to has been discussed variously under rubrics like *thematic roles/relations, Case theory* (not morphological case or the abstract CASE of GB-theories, but rather the semantic cases of Fillmore and others), *theta-theory (θ-theory),* and so on. I use the term *thematic-roles.* Some typical examples of such roles are Agent, Patient or Theme, Instrument, Goal, Source, and so on, as illustrated in these sentences:

18. Sally gave the book to Bill.
19. John opened the door with a crowbar.
20. The door opened.
21. I bought the book from James.

In sentence 18, Sally is the Agent; the book is the Theme in that sentence as well as in example 21; Bill is the Goal. In sentence 19, John is the Agent; the door is the theme; the Instrument is a crowbar. In sentence 20, there is no Agent, but the door is still the Theme. In sentence 21, I am the Agent, James is the Source. Semantically, thematic roles seem to represent generalizations that we make across different kinds of happenings in the world about the participation of individuals in the eventualities that the various sentences are about. (In GB-theory, θ-roles serve a very syntactic purpose; their specific semantic content seems to play no part at all.)

One can observe two important things about thematic roles. First, they are not to be confused with purely grammatical relations like those we call Subject, Object, Indirect Object, and so on, although there is obviously some connection between these two ways of looking at what noun phrases are doing in sentences. In example 19, *John* is the Subject as is *the door* in example 20, but I have said that the door is the Theme in both sentences.

Notice what is presupposed in the way I put this last sentence: grammatical relations have to do with expressions in a sentence; thematic roles have to do with the things that they denote (this is not an uncontroversial assumption). Important generalizations can be made (such as those of Fillmore, 1968) about the way in which thematic roles are expressed via grammatical relation, as illustrated in these sentences:

(19) John opened the door with a crowbar.
(20) The door opened.
22. A crowbar opened the door.
23. ??The door opened with a crowbar.

Second, the semantic contents associated with thematic roles verge off into essentially philosophical issues about the nature of human action, responsibility, volition, causation, and so on. *A priori,* we might expect a good deal of cultural variation in these areas. To the extent that theories of thematic relations seem to have some language-independent validity, it seems that we are getting at important semantic universals about how humans understand the world and classify actions, events, and the participation of individuals in them. In other words, we seem again to be getting into the realm of natural language metaphysics. Moreover, just as with the theory of eventualities, to pursue these questions we must study the meanings of individual lexical elements.

Once again, I have neither the time nor the space here to follow out these questions in detail, which (as I indicated previously) are just beginning to be taken up seriously in model-theoretic approaches to meaning. Let me just sketch one way of incorporating thematic roles into a semantic theory for natural language, which seem to be ready-make to help us flesh out the connections between different kinds of things in our model structure.

We can expect two important contributions from the incorporation of thematic roles into our interpretations. First, they give us a further handle on noting and characterizing differences among different kinds of things in our model structures. One of the major differences between "ordinary" objects and properties-as-individuals lies in the lack of expected thematic roles for the former type and the regularity of their presence for the latter. John Smith requires no Agent or Theme. Kissings require both. This fact is correlated with another one in a completely regular way. The propositional function or predicate of which Kissing is the individual correlate is a two-place relation, so a systematic relation exists between the number of slots or "places" that a predicate has and the number of thematic roles regularly associated with it. (This fact is reflected in the "θ-criterion" of GB theories. This criterion ensures a one-one relation between "argument" positions and θ-roles, where we have to bear in mind that "argument" is used in a special technical way within that theory.)

How might we incorporate thematic relations into a model-theoretic semantics? The most natural way, or so it seems to me, is to exploit the relationship between arguments of predicates and thematic roles we have just noted and to provide meaning postulates that spell out the thematic roles that are to be associated with each predicate. A syntactic view would be to think of each role as a function from predicates to positions or expressions standing in those positions. A semantic account, on the other hand, would be telling us something about the entities involved in a relation. Therefore, for a predicate such as *kiss,* a meaning postulate will tell us that if *a* stands in the *kiss* relation to *b,* then *a* has the Agent role and *b* the Patient role in the situation (which equals world) in which the kissing takes place. Because these roles are (or are given by) functions, one-half of the θ-criterion is automatic. The other half—which says (syntactically speaking) that each argument position can be associated with at most one thematic role—seems to be just wrong (semantically, at least), as evidenced by the relationship between pairs of sentences such as:

    24. John kissed Sally.
    25. John kissed himself.

The introduction of events (and other kinds of eventualities) as elements in the model structure, whether primitive or constructed, owes a great deal to the work of Donald Davidson, who argued persuasively for such a move in a series of papers first published in the 1960s. Among the important questions he raised was one about the identification of events. Suppose I am driving a car and raise my left arm to feel whether a load on the roof of my car is still secure. Someone behind me sees this event and interprets it as a signal for a right turn. Did I signal a right turn, even inadvertently? Questions of this sort arise often in courts of law. Or suppose I shoot a gun at a cardboard target, unaware that someone is standing behind the target, and as a result the person behind the target dies. Is there some sense in which my shooting the gun at the target and my (accidentally) killing the person are the same event? As I have described it, we surely have to say that even though the shooting was quite deliberate on my part the killing was unintentional. I may very well be accused of carelessness but scarcely of murder. These examples recall strongly the puzzle about the ring and the gold (example 6), and we can use the same kind of solution here: the killing and the shooting might be "materially identical" in the sense that they are mapped into the very same manifestation or "stuff" but still distinct. So the setup we are exploring here provides the possibility of analyzing what we mean when we talk about "events under a description."

I have dwelt at some length on Cresswell's analysis of worlds because I think it offers a rather fruitful way of looking at some of the problems we have been considering and also because I think the analysis has been undeservedly neglected. It incorporates a way of talking about "little worlds," which has been a feature of another theory, which is much more recent, and to which I now turn for a brief discussion.

As the name suggests, *situation semantics* as developed by Barwise and Perry in the last several years, takes the notion of a situation as very basic. Intuitively we can think of a situation in much the way we have been talking in the last discussion. On the other hand, unlike all the theories I have addressed thus far, situation semantics doe not use the notion of a possible world at all. Another respect in which situation semantics departs from many previous semantic theories in the model-theoretic tradition is that sentences do not denote truth-values but rather "describe" situations in some sense to be made precise. The idea that sentences denote truth-values has a venerable history in modern logic and philosophy of language; again, Frege is perhaps the most important name in this tradition. Of course, Frege associated another kind of object with sentences (as their "senses"), namely, the proposition. We have explored a bit Montague's reconstruction of the proposition as a function from worlds (and times) to truth-values (equivalently, as a set of worlds), and we have also briefly discussed some of the problems of this notion: the identity of all necessarily true propositions and so on. As a first approximation, we can say that in situation semantics, ordinary declarative sentences can be taken to denote sets of situations, the situations in which they are true.

An extended exposition of the technical apparatus that was developed (and is still being developed) by the proponents of situation semantics is not feasible here, but here are a few highlights.

Situations as such—what we might call *real* situations—do not appear in the theory at all. Instead, certain kinds of things—individuals, relations, (space-time) locations—are abstracted out of real situations and put back together into abstract objects of various kinds, which may be thought of as ways to classify and model real situations. Among these abstract objects, perhaps the most important one is the situation-type. A *situation type* is: a partial function from relations and individuals to truth-values; equivalently: an ordered sequence consisting of an n-place relation, n individuals, and a truth-value. Relations such as Chierchia's properties) are to be thought of not as ordered n-tuples of individuals but as real independent things in the model-structure. The partiality of the function is important: for a given situation (or location) a situation-type may represent the fact that the individuals do stand in the relation named or that they do not. Another situation-type for the same situation may simply say nothing about the situation. Consequently, partiality comes into the semantics in two ways: First, the very notion of a situation corresponds intuitively to something we might think of as a restricted subpart of a world (much like Cresswell's "little" worlds); second, situation-types (among other things in the theory) as partial function allow us to reconstruct the circumstance in which we only have quite incomplete information about something or other—that is, the circumstance that we normally or always face. (In my last lecture I looked briefly at another kind of model-theory, which is designed to cope with partiality in a radically different way.)

Partiality is rightly held to be one of the essential ways in which situation semantics departs from Montague's possible worlds semantics. Let me illustrate one point about partiality, which will also serve to lead into the last topic of this lecture. Very often we seem to want to be able to talk about the individuals that are involved in some limited situation; that is, those individuals comprising some very partial subdomain of the big domain of all possible individuals that we take as given in advance in a standard model structure. Why can't we just literally take the individuals that are "in" some such limited situation and confine our attention to them? Well, the problem is that in this way of thinking of situations, situations are still "thick" or "dense"; just too much is still going on in them, if we take them quite literally. Consider the room we are in right now over a little stretch of time: what are the individuals that are in it, ALL of them? There are all the people, all the clothes that they are wearing, all the tables and chairs, all the nails and screws that are in them, all the hairs on my head, the molecules comprising them, the electrons and neutrons, ... But that is just beginning: what about all the plural individuals that Link has bequeathed us: my left ear plus one of the hairs on my head, that hair plus another hair, . . . and so on and so on. For purposes of semantics, we want to ignore most of these possibilities and focus just on some relevant subset of this plethora of individuals. Things like situation-types allow us to isolate as small a set of individuals as we want to have available for linguistic purposes: we can work with a well-defined set of individuals in a situation by appeal to the situation-types that do represent or model the real situation in a very partial way.

Before turning to my last topic for today, I want to address the real difficulties that arise when you try to work out the details of the sorts of theories we've been looking at. Many people seem to agree that we want to be able to deal with situations, things like worlds but "smaller" than worlds as usually understood and entering into some sort of ordering or part-whole relation. Several difficult problems must be dealt with, and I have not addressed them. One problem is that of negation. In classical possible world semantics, negation is quite straightforward; in models such as those we have been looking at it is very difficult (Barwise and Perry (1983), for example, simply does not treat sentence negation). Another problem is that of so-called *persistence*. If a statement is true relative to a certain restricted situation, what happens when we extend the situation to larger ones "containing" it? We can call a sentence (or sentence meaning) persistent in a situation if it is true under all extensions of the situation. We certainly want all logically true statements to be persistent in this sense. But what about contingent sentences, that is, those that depend upon the facts? Again a difficult problem (see Kratzer, forthcoming).

The theories I have been focussing on today still conform more or less to the general structure of model theoretic semantic theories: we have a language, a model-structure, and a function or relation from one to the other. The last theories I will bring up today—and I can do no more than mention them—alter this setup fundamentally. These are theories of Irene Heim and Hans Kamp that make the interpretation of a language a two-stage process. Heim's theory is called *file change semantics;* Kamp's, *discourse representation theory*. They were developed independently at about the same time and differ in important and interesting ways, but they share this one feature. I will talk mainly about Heim's theory.

The theories were developed originally to deal with a number of problems about quantification and anaphora that remain unsolved in the standard theory. We can see one of these problems in the famous "donkey"-sentences discussed originally in the medieval period and brought to the attention of modern thinkers by Peter Geach (1962):

26. Every farmer who owns a donkey beats it.

The problem has to do with the way in which we relate the pronoun *it* to its antecedent *a donkey*. We can notice the problem by observing that in Montague's theory about English in *PTQ,* the only way to get this anaphoric relation is to derive the sentence by quantifying in *a donkey*. Two problems arise with this derivation: first, it gives the sentence the wrong meaning; second, there are strong constraints on the syntactic contexts into which we can carry out such quantifying-in-and-binding operations that would be violated even to get the wrong interpretation that *PTQ* makes available. We can see the operation of these constraints in a sentence that is parallel to 26:

27. ?A donkey who loves every farmer kicks him.

(Here *him* is supposed to be linked to *every farmer*.) And the wrong meaning that this illegitimate derivation would produce is paraphrased as sentence 28:

28. There is a donkey that every farmer who owns it beats.

Somehow, sentence 26 does not seem to be about some particular donkey that every farmer owns, but rather about all owner-donkey pairs. What to do?

An examination of this and similar problems led both Heim and Kamp to a far-reaching revision of the structure of a semantic theory for a natural language. Both theories proceed by interposing a theory of *discourses* between the expressions of a language and the model or world which ultimately determines the truth and falsity (and so on) of the expressions.

Consider this simple example of a discourse with two participants and how it is handled in Heim's theory:

29. A: There's a donkey in the garden.
    B: It belongs to a woman who lives next door.
    A: Does she know that it is in our garden?

This mini-discourse illustrates how a conversation can be used to build up and ask questions about a fund of information that is the subject matter of the discourse. We imagine that the two speakers are engaged in a common enterprise that we may think of as creating a file of information. Some of the aspects of this file draw upon a common basis that the speakers share as an initial state in the conversation. Others are created as the conversation proceeds. In the first sentence, A introduces a certain entity into the discourse and gives two pieces of information about it: that it is a donkey and that it is in the garden. The use of the indefinite article *a* signals the fact that the donkey in question is being newly introduced as an entity. We can imagine that the participants take a fresh file card, write down a previously unused number on it, add the information given in the first sentence to it and put the card into a box. What information? One piece is unproblematic: the new entity is a donkey. The other piece—that the donkey is in the garden— requires a bit more work. The use of the definite article *the* indicates that there should already "be a card" relating to a garden—either from a common background of information or from previous discourse. Here the participants check the file to find a card and enter into it the information that the entity associated with the new card (the donkey card) is in the entity associated with the garden card. (If no such card is found, then by a process known as *accommodation* the participants supply a card "as if it were already there"). In the subsequent sentences this same process is repeated: a new card for the woman next door, updating the donkey card to add the information about the information about ownership, and so on. Finally, the last question explicitly invites an action that will continue this process one way or another according to a true answer to the question.

I do not want to go into the technical apparatus needed to spell out this procedure formally (see Heim's work for details), but two points are of special interest to us here. First, given this setup, we can then go on to talk about truth or falsity of a discourse on the basis of a correspondence between the *a file* and *a world*. A discourse file is true if it can be related to a world in a truthful way: a donkey really is in the garden, etc. Second, indefinite and definite descriptions are understood not in quantificational terms but in terms of directives for updating a file, adding new cards, and so on.

We can now return to the problematical donkey-sentences (such as sentence 26) and explain them in terms of truth-preserving extensions of files: for every farmer and donkey pair satisfying the conditions of the first part of the sentence, a true extension satisfying the second part of the sentence exists. Consequently, here, too, the quantificational force of *every* is removed from the sentence and reconstructed in terms of growths of discourse files. (At the level of generality at which we are discussing this theory, very little must be modified to give an account of Kamp's discourse representation theory.)

In this lecture, we have looked at a number of recent directions in current research, all of which share a common theme: a search for model structures that contain in one way or another world-like structures that are more flexible and potentially "smaller" than the maximal worlds of the classical theories. I have also tried to relate some of these newer approaches to each other and to topics we have dealt with in previous lectures. I have to emphasize that my discussion has been all too sketchy and that any of the topics of the lecture could easily have formed the basis for several more lectures. If I have whetted your appetite, so that you go out with the intention of finding out more about these topics, then I will consider the lecture successful.

Lecture VIII:

ODDS AND ENDINGS

The topics I will address today fall into two major classes: one has to do with the nature of the semantic objects we have been dealing with and how they might relate to things that people might talk about under different conceptions of semantics as an enterprise; the other has to do with the relationship between semantics and syntax, and also other sorts of realms (pragmatics, knowledge about the world, beliefs, and so on). I am going to take up these matters in the form of giving answers to questions that have been raised by some of you to me and to questions that you might have raised and did not.

Q: In the first lecture you mentioned that there are other approaches to semantics that are not model-theoretic. Would you please say something about them and how they relate to what you have been talking about?

A: This question touches on one of the most difficult problems about the enterprise of semantics, and it leads us into some very interesting additional questions.

Since Chomsky's earliest influence on the field, many linguists (not all!) have accepted the idea that linguistic theory is best thought of as a branch of cognitive psychology, the general field concerned with understanding people's mental abilities. In our ruminations about semantics thus far, we have not thought at all about the mind. We have talked about languages and things that the expressions denote: truth-values, individuals, properties, and so on, and we have helped ourselves to things such as worlds and times and all sorts of mathematical functions and relations to try to approach a satisfying answer to the question we started from. What is a meaning?

Suppose we now want to think about a psychological theory about semantics—what we might call *psychosemantics*. Could we sensibly think about these semantic objects we have been happily talking about as some sort of mental objects? (Let us not get distracted by an important and difficult side issue: does it make any sense to talk about "mental" objects? I am perfectly happy if you believe that all talk about mental objects, thoughts, concepts, and so on, is just a disguised way of talking about things that are ultimately composed of physical things and their relations. In that case, we can defend talk about the mental as a necessary reorganization of the units of discussion when we reach a certain level of complexity.)

A quick answer would be: No, they cannot possibly literally *be* mental objects because there are too many of them and they are too big. We can't have worlds in our heads, not to speak of individuals like John and then all of the functions, functions on functions, and so on, that even relatively modest model-structures come furnished with. So consequently, we might want to refine the question a bit: do we have in our heads mental objects of some kind that correspond to or represent some or all of the things we have been talking about? For example, it might make sense to think that we have a (psychological) concept of horses that corresponds in some way to the property Horse in our semantics, however that is understood. Then we might ask what the relationship is between these two things: the concept of horses and the property Horse.

There is an important line of argument (due chiefly to Hilary Putnam) which has urged that whatever this relationship is, it is not anything near to identity. Take Montague's notion of a property as a function from world-time pairs to sets: in this case, sets of horses. In standard model-theoretic semantics, such a property is taken to be a certain thing that gives us very definite answers to questions such as: "Is Abraham a horse?" Such a view seems to carry with it the idea that the property should provide us with necessary and sufficient criteria for determining whether something is a horse. And people just do not possess such criteria for most of the things which they talk about. Much philosophical discussion has occurred about this matter and all the other questions that arise: What about worlds where there is something that has all the properties of water in our world but is chemically distinct from it (and is called *water* in this other world)? Or what if we discovered that what we call *cats* (and believe to be natural animals) turned out to be cleverly designed robots controlled by invisible beings from another planet? Would they still be cats? Or suppose there were a pencil tree, the fruits or nuts of which were indistinguishable from pencils as we know and love them, would these things really be pencils? It is fun and instructive to think about such questions. Personally, I tend to agree with people who say that we use language in a sort of "as-if" mode: we use the concept of horses with the silent understanding that the things we call horses are horses according to whatever the "correct" understanding of this concept should be. There is an inescapable modal or intentional aspect to our understanding of such concepts. (Notice the same problem really occurs with ordinary individuals: will the real John Jones please stand up!) Putnam has stressed the importance of cooperative social aspects of meaning: we defer to experts who know more about horses, gold, water, etc. than we do.

I cannot give a better answer to the question here than that. Let me just reiterate: I think the best way to think about this question is to frame it as a question about mental representations or concepts and their relationship to the kinds of (nonmental) things we talk about in our semantic theories. Incidentally, Heim's and Kamp's theories which we looked at all too briefly in the last lecture are very relevant here: discourse representations and files seem to lend themselves very nicely to the task of thinking about the necessarily partial representations that we might have in our heads.

Q: One thing bothers me about the semantic theories you have been talking about: they seem to assume sharp borderlines to kinds of things. Something is either in a set or it is not. In a lot of our talk—maybe most of it—we operate with concepts or whatever that simply are not like that: Is Mr. So-and-So tall? Is this object red? Is this thing a piece of furniture? When does a chair get wide enough to be called a couch? And so on.

A: Your question raises the very important problem of vagueness or indeterminacy in the meanings of words. You are obviously right in what you say.

First of all, let me say that one can give an answer in terms of strategies of research. We cannot do everything at once and we always operate under conditions of some kind of idealization. So we might defend what we are doing by saying that we can pretend a preciseness that we have to admit we do not really have and see how far we can get toward understanding the *structure* of meanings of natural languages under this simplifying assumption. I think that is a reasonable move, but in a way it is just postponing the problem.

Assuming that we do want to face the problem, we will probably want to separate cases. As often happens, it turns out that many different problems are lumped together under one heading, and it makes sense to treat them in different ways. Let me illustrate.

1. Some animals have kidneys.

This sentence is true. Suppose ALL animals had kidneys (I think that's false), would sentence 1 be false? Logic says no (as long as there are some animals). But ordinary usage is such that we wonder whether in Language (as opposed to Logic) we want to say that sentence 1 should be true or false (in this hypothetical situation where all animals have kidneys). I think it is quite defensible to say that semantics should follow Logic here and account for the way we ordinarily use and understand sentences such as example 1 by a different theory, for example a theory of the "logic" of conversation, conventional and conversational implicatures and the like, such as the one put forward by Paul Grice. Similar remarks could be made about the way we use *or*, *if*, and so on. This is one kind of case.

2. Mr. So-and-So is tall.

Suppose Mr. So-and-So is a professional basketball player. Then if he's two meters tall, we might be inclined to say that sentence 2 isn't true. But supposes he's a CHILD professional basketball player (assuming such things existed), then we might change our minds. Here, I think we want to say that words such as tall implicitly carry with them a standard of comparison, which can be made explicit in English by adding *for a basketball player* or whatever. That's another kind of case, where we can sharpen up our understanding a bit by spelling out more exactly what such a word means.

But still, you might say, even if we pin down the meaning of *tall* in some such way, doesn't an inescapable element of vagueness remain in the meaning of the word? I think the answer is yes. There is a famous puzzle (called *Sorites*) based on this sort of vagueness. Suppose we agree that a man is short if he is one meter tall. Suppose we further agree that if a man is short and if you added .001 millimeters to his height he would still be short. If you accept those two assumptions, then you can "prove" that a man three meters tall is short.

Thinking about such puzzles and similar matters has led people to develop "theories of vagueness," which are precise ways of building vagueness into a theory of meaning. For example, Hans Kamp has devoted quite a bit of thought to such problems and proposed a theory where we relativize the understanding of some words to contexts and say something similar to this: relative to some degree of precision we segregate the denotation of some word X into three cases: definitely X, definitely *not-X*, and indeterminate (that is, somewhere in-between). As you might guess, this sort of theory leads to thinking about systems with "truth-value gaps" or three-valued logics (True, False, Undefined—recall our discussions of sortal incorrectness in Lecture V).

Another interesting set of considerations I will mention briefly arises, I think, from reflections on meaning by the philosopher Ludwig Wittgenstein. Wittgenstein argued that the meanings of most or many words should really be thought of as quite indeterminate. If you ask someone what a game is (his example), that person might name some typical games, and say "Games are things like that." If you pressed this person for real criteria for what counts as a game, he or she might be at a loss. Do games require winning and losing? Well, a lot do, but then what about playing jump rope? And so on. A lot of psychological research has been done on such notions, usually under the name of *prototypes*, and Putnam has also picked up on this idea in his efforts to think about meaning in a way that gets away from ideas of definite functions. There are currently efforts to try to see how one might incorporate such ideas into a formal-semantic framework.

Finally, let me just mention a current line of thought that involves a much more wholesale rethinking or refinement of standard model-theoretic semantics. In standard approaches, questions about *knowledge* never enter into the picture. People who are beginning to study model-theoretic semantics are often troubled by this fact: How do you *know* that such and such is true? We quickly learn to separate out some questions as questions about epistemology. We assume we know and then see what follows. So, in a way, standard approaches provide a sort of "semantics for God," an all-knowing being. But, in fact, we always operate with partial and possibly quite wrong ideas about what is the case. Would not it be instructive to face this situation more squarely and develop a semantic theory based not on (presumed) total knowledge but rather on the notion of partial knowledge and thinking formally about the process of increasing knowledge? Then we might think of a standard semantics as providing a kind of limiting case. Given a theory about partial information and growth of information, then leaping to the situation where the information becomes complete (which it most likely will not for us) would give us "God's semantics." This direction is exactly the one that is being pursued currently under the name of *data semantics* (Landman, 1986; Veltman, 1985). The theory is especially relevant to understanding some of the persistent puzzles about modality and the semantics of conditional sentences.

Again, I cannot do much more than invite you to visit this new theory. As with some of the approaches mentioned in the last lecture, the theory depends crucially on the use of partial functions. *Partial functions* are functions from some domain that yield values only for a subset of the objects in the domain. If the function does not yield a value for some argument in the domain, we say that the value is "undefined." But what does "undefined" mean? Data semantics takes the view that this could very well mean something like this: undetermined as far as the current state of knowledge is concerned, but possibly to be determined as knowledge grows. Then, we get a natural ordering of functions based on partiality of information and study ways in which functions "settle down" to a state where no further information can change them.

Q: You promised that you would say something about the relation between semantics and other parts of a bigger theory of language: syntax, pragmatics, and, perhaps, other areas as well.

A: Thank you for reminding me. Let me concentrate first on *syntax*, understood in the broadest way to include not only theories about the structure of sentences and other sorts of phrases but going down into questions about word structure, what is traditionally called *morphology*. Then I will return to some of the areas that are more closely connected to what we conventionally think of as meaning.

As I think has been evident from various places in these lectures, Montague's general theory provided a very tight relationship between syntax and semantics. First of all, there is in that theory a functional relationship between the syntactic categories and the semantic types of his intentional logic and hence the types of objects in the model structure. In Lecture V, we took note of some of the problems that view leads to and we noted there and later that one way of dealing with those problems is to make some fundamental changes in the model-structure, either by sorting the domain, or enriching *and* simplifying it as in the property-theoretic approaches of Chierchia and others. Second, a very close relation is supposed to exist between the *rules* of the syntax and the *rules* of the semantics, and we contrasted this view—the *rule-to-rule* hypothesis—with the configurational theories of, for example, GB theory.

I think there is a great deal to be said for exploring this tightly constrained sort of relationship as a research strategy. We might contrast it with a "straw" theory, which places no constraints at all on the relationship between syntax and semantics. In the latter sort of approach, nothing at all about the ways in which various meanings are expressed in natural languages would be surprising. We want theories that have a lot of "surprise value," that is, that make a lot of specific predictions about the domain of inquiry. That way we are more likely to find out that they are wrong, and knowledge advances by uncovering error. By the way, I think we have to treat this aspect of our theory like any other: hypotheses that we are exploring and testing and not some kind of *a priori* constraint on admissible analyses.

Tightly constrained theories about the relationship between syntax and semantics are severely strained in several places. One such place is in the functional correspondence idea about syntactic categories and semantic types. Consider, for example, noun phrases. Traditionally, linguists have often drawn a distinction between predicative and nonpredicative noun phrases, as in these contrasts:

3. An anthropologist appeared at the door.
4. Ms. Jones is an anthropologist.
5. I consider Ms. Jones an anthropologist.

In sentences 4 and 5, *an anthropologist* is being used as a predicate nominal, in contrast to sentence 3. Semantically, we might want to say that in the predicative use the noun phrases are not generalized quantifiers at all but rather some sort of predicates (for example, therefore, sentence 4 would be represented in PC just like this *Anthropologist(mj)*, where *mj* stands for Ms. Jones). But if that is right and if we want to say that the predicate nominals are noun phrases—and such phrases generally exhibit all the internal characteristics of noun phrases—then the functional correspondence principle seems to be threatened. A very fruitful dispute about just this point has occurred between Edwin Williams and Barbara Partee. The result has been a suggested relaxation of the correspondence principle but not an abandonment of it: it seems that there are systematic and predictable variations of noun-phrase meanings. The suggested modification of the correspondence principle in this case also leads to some interesting predictions about what particular noun phrases can function predicatively and in what circumstances, as illustrated by these further examples from the Williams–Partee interchange:

6. ?Ms. Jones is every anthropologist.
7. This house has been every color.

(It is worth thinking about the possibility that sentence 6 is odd because it is so likely to be false. But even if there is only one anthropologist it still seems odd). The solution proposed for the problem of predicate nominals is also relevant to another set of problems about noun phrases that come up when we consider conjunctions of various sorts of verbal expressions:

8. Mary hugged and kissed a bystander.
9. Mary wanted and bought a hat.

We want to be able to say that if sentence 8 is true then there was a bystander that Mary hugged and kissed, but for sentence 9 we do not want to say that there was necessarily a particular hat that Mary wanted and bought. Partee suggests that noun phrases have a very particular range of possible interpretations that are systematically related: as individuals, as properties or predicates, or as generalized quantifiers. The point I want to make here is that it is only if we start from a fairly constrained theory about the mapping from syntax to semantics that such problems are problems. Looking for solutions then leads to interesting and systematic modifications of the theory, not to a wholesale abandonment of it.

Incidentally, this might be an appropriate point to interject a remark about research strategies in semantics. I have stressed in the last few lectures new directions that are taking the tack of modifying or extending the "classical" sort of possible worlds semantics that Montague used. It is important to realize that possible worlds semantics is alive and well and that some researchers are doing a very good job of pushing the approach as far as it will go and trying to think about the difficult problems that have been posed (propositional attitudes, for example) and ways of dealing with them that do not necessarily involve abandoning the very real virtues of the classical approach (Cresswell (1985) and Stalnaker (1984) are two good examples). You do not always want to throw away things that you have when something new comes along.

I called the theory I was contrasting with Montague's here a "straw" theory, or a kind of "straw man" approach. I doubt that anyone seriously espouses such a theory. Real disagreements exist about the nature of semantics and the way in which people should try to spell out the relationship between semantics and syntax. This diversity is to be welcomed, in my opinion, and should be discussed and explored in a cooperative spirit.

I cannot leave this topic without putting in a little "plug" for a family of theories of syntax that focuses squarely on the syntax-semantics relationship: so-called *categorial theories*. Montague used categorial theories of syntax in part in *PTQ*. They have been around for quite a while, but with sporadic exceptions have not been pursued all that much by linguists. In the last few years a revival of interest has occurred in these theories. One of their central features has been a dogged insistence on the centrality of functions and arguments in language, both in syntax and in semantics.

So much for syntax. Let me add a few remarks on other parts of a big theory about language. First, with regard to aspects of meaning in the broad sense that we've neglected, an important part of meaning has to do with the way information is conveyed. I am thinking of the things that are traditionally treated under the heading of focus and background, new information versus old, and so on. In various languages, such matters are often conveyed by the use of special markers or constructions, by word order, and by intonation and emphatic stress. Although Heim's and Kamp's theories that we looked at in the last lecture are potentially very relevant to such questions, a lot more must be taken into account. Provisionally, we might think of this as another way of organizing the meaning of expressions, and a task of a more nearly complete theory of meaning would be to investigate how this kind of structure relates to the sort of meaning we have been talking about in terms of denotational structures. A second area I have barely mentioned is that of presuppositions or implicatures. These two areas of meaning are intimately related. Very often, two utterances that may not be truth-conditionally distinct can vary in the presuppositions that they convey, depending on intonation, for example. Finally—not "finally" in the absolute sense, of course, but only in the sense that it is the last thing I will treat about meaning proper—there are all kinds of "meaning" that have to do with the setting of language uses: contextual information about the speaker and hearer, their attitudes to each other, and social matters, not to mention attitudes toward the subject matter of discourses. For example, in some languages obligatory differences are found between words used by men and women.

Most of what I have addressed in these lectures has been on the level of language competence; that is, trying to give an account of what language users know in some implicit way (with the important qualifications we have considered today about the psychological side of semantics). When we use and understand language, we bring to bear on these tasks a lot of general knowledge, in addition to many cognitive abilities that are probably involved in many nonlinguistic abilities as well. In semantics, there is always a question about the line between general knowledge about the world and semantics proper. Workers in artificial intelligence appreciate more than most of the rest of us, I think, the huge role that world knowledge plays in language and other cognitive domains.

Q: You have told us a lot about some very abstract theories about natural language semantics. Do these theories have any practical applications?

A: Another excellent but difficult question. I do not feel the need to justify the pursuit of knowledge of any kind you might mention by the possible practical applications it might have, and I will not assume you were presupposing the need for such justification when you asked that question. For me, it is enough to say this: Here is a phenomenon (like a mountain for the mountainclimber), it is there so I want to understand it (mountainclimber: climb it). History shows science progresses best by taking this attitude as a primary reason. But, of course, societies have to ask about practical effects, good or bad, that might result from scientific activity. Furthermore, history also shows, I think, that scientific understanding does sometimes come from trying to tackle practical problems. Finally, again and again it has turned out that some area of knowledge has some practical applications or effects that were never dreamed of by the people who developed it. One famous example is the development of non-Euclidian geometries, which were thought of initially as purely abstract structures that just turned out to be conceivable after it was realized that one of Euclid's axioms was independent of the others and that you could drop or replace it and see what happened. These geometries turned out then to be crucial for relativity theory, and most of us know about some of the practical and serious consequences of that theory. Another example is prime-number theory and the mathematics of very large numbers, which are now of immense importance for cryptography.

That said, what about practical applications of model theoretic semantics in particular? Well, I am not going to be very sanguine. One can ask the same question about theoretical linguistics in general. Potentially practical applications could be found, but the easy ones to think of are fraught with difficulty. For example, many of you are language teachers. Does linguistics help you in your tasks? Probably in a general way, if it helps you understand the structure of languages, gives you some insight into how languages can differ, and so on. But we cannot derive anything directly from linguistic theory about language teaching. That requires putting TWO theories together, at least, one about language and one about learning. Formal semantics has had some impact on computer science: trying to say something precise about the semantics of programs has turned out to be very difficult and some workers have drawn on ideas from model-theoretic semantics, but this is an area I am not competent to address.

Q: Would you say something about current directions in semantics and what we can expect to be the important lines of research in the next few years?

A: This is a good question to end on. First, I have already said a good deal about current directions of research. The main point of these lectures has been to introduce you to enough of the technical apparatus of model-theoretic semantics for me to go on to say something about the exciting work that is being conducted in this field today. The areas I have touched on that are currently being pursued include the study of generalized quantifiers, various experiments with modified model-structures like the property-theories of Chierchia and others, the use of intermediate levels of interpretations as in Heim's and Kamp's theories, and other more radical reworkings of the whole foundations of semantics like data semantics and situation semantics.

What about the future? Well, I expect that all the things I have just mentioned will continue to be pursued and modified in the coming years. Perhaps the best thing I could do here would be to talk about some problems that need to be looked at or solved as well as some areas where there seems to be some convergence of opinion among workers in different frameworks.

Psychosemantics. What kind of semantic representations do people actually have in their heads? I have already mentioned some of the issues that arise when we ask questions like this. Serious approaches to such questions obviously have to involve psychologists and psycholinguists as well as semanticists. I suspect that the next few years will see some progress on such topics, and judging from the past we can expect a lot of vigorous debate. I hope more interaction will occur between the kind of model-theoretic approaches exemplified in the work we have surveyed here and other kinds of approaches. Let me just cite one example of a topic of current interest.

One problem about doing research on semantics is that great difficulties arise when determining just what the data is that you are trying to account for. In general, we deal in linguistics with native speakers judgments: Is a sentence acceptable, ungrammatical? What is the plural for a specific word? The data can get very messy. The kinds of judgments that we have to ask about in semantics often seem to be very shaky: How many ways ambiguous is a certain sentence with several quantified noun-phrases in it? Does a certain sentence entail another sentence? Many people seem very unsure about their judgments about such matters. It often seems as if people have to go through some kind of a separate process to come to some kind of conclusion (if any!) about logical properties of sentences. A typical kind of question would be posed by a sentence such as this one:

    10. Many arrows did not hit a target.

Can this sentence be used to describe a situation in which all the arrows in question hit some target or other but there was one target that many arrows missed?

    Some people would like to say that when we understand a sentence such as example 10 we usually just compute a semantic representation that is "neutral" or "unspecified" as far as the scope of the quantifier expressions and the negation is concerned, and that it is only a later separate kind of processing that we go through (sometimes!) to figure out the scope possibilities. Thus far, however, no one has managed to come up with a good representational system for such a neutral or unspecified representation that does not amount to computing all the scope possibilities and then summing over them. Here, I hope that further study would try to connect up with the very interesting research that Philip Johnson-Laird has done on how people reason. (Johnson-Laird believes that people make little "mental models" that they use for reasoning, see the book of that title in the references.)

    Probably, the research in "psychosemantics" that I expect to take place will coordinate with work in artificial intelligence, when people try to build computer models of various kinds of human cognitive processes (although I am not very sanguine about the results, as yet). But this work has to be genuinely committed to the development of real theories. It is very seductive when you have written a program that simulates some kind of human behavior to think that what you have constitutes a theory, just by virtue of the fact that it works (if it really does!). Computers are computers and people are people. The computer metaphor has been very fruitful in cognitive psychology, but it is just a metaphor unless you are able to build some fairly tight theoretical links between what the computer does and what you think people do.

    Events etc. It has probably been pretty apparent that I myself am very interested in all the topics we have discussed in the last few lectures under the headings of "verbal aspect," situations, and so on. Here there has been a very interesting tie-in between work by a variety of different linguists, working under frameworks as diverse as GB theory, situation semantics, and

Montague grammar, and work by philosophers. I expect we are just at the beginning of work of this kind now. I could just as well have mentioned this area under the last heading also, because I think it is obvious here that we are going beyond the realm of linguistics proper and have to bring in work about other conceptual domains. Ray Jackendoff has written quite explicitly about this point in a recent book (1983) and has also led the way to bringing in evidence about theories of vision to questions about semantic and other conceptual structures. In my opinion, an important link can be made here to much earlier work on the perception of causality and so on by the psychologist Michotte and his coworkers. (Closely related to this work will be, I think, a continuation of thought about thematic relations as substantive parts of semantic theories.)

At various points in these lectures we have ended up with questions that seem to verge off into matters I have called natural language metaphysics. Again (as you might guess) this topic is dear to my heart. It relates most directly to some of the biggest and most difficult questions that we face. Most ordinary people are not very interested in much of the technical work that linguists do. But many of them have heard at one time or other of the so-called *Sapir-Whorf hypothesis* (the idea that our languages determine the most basic patterns of our thought), or they have themselves come up with similar ideas as they reflect on their own linguistic experience. As teachers of linguistics, we often have a problem about this. Students come into our courses burning with curiosity about this and other very basic questions about language. Such students are often disappointed when they learn that a great deal of linguistics is concerned with rather arcane and abstract systems that seem to be very far away from these interesting BIG questions. "Language is a window to the mind!" we say in our advertisements for our courses. "What do we see through this window?" they eagerly ask. The syntactician says: "Lots of very unusual principles that have no relevance to anything outside of language." The semanticist says: "Functions from possible worlds to functions from individual concepts to truth values." (Big deal!) Still, I feel that we are today in a much better position than we were a few decades ago for taking up some of these old Big Questions again. And we should by all means.

Let me close by inviting you to take part in this search for new answers to old questions and in the uncovering of new questions about old answers. It is an exciting search and cannot be done without the help of many people in many lands. I thank you for your interest and for the opportunity to talk with you.

NOTES

LECTURE I

A classic and nicely general plea for the model-theoretic approach to semantics is Lewis (1972), reprinted in Partee (1976). Dowty, Wall, and Peters (1981) is a detailed introduction to Montague semantics. Montague's theories about language and natural language were set forth in several papers included in Montague (1974), which has itself an introduction to Montague's work by the editor Richmond Thomason. Montague's general theory of language is given in his paper "Universal Grammar" (Paper 7 in Montague, 1974); his best-known paper, which forms the basis for most of the material in the next few lectures is "The Proper Treatment of Quantification in Ordinary English" (*PTQ:* Paper 8 in the same place). Fodor (1977) is an introduction to various approaches to semantics within the program of generative grammar. The best book on the whole field of formal semantics for natural language is Gamut (1982). A concise introduction to Montague's work on semantics, which is unusual in its extensive reliance on and explications of Montague's general theory, is Link (1979).

LECTURE II

The main references for the material in this lecture are the same as for the first lecture. Linsky (1971) is a useful collection of older papers on modality including Kripke's classic paper from 1963. The possible worlds analysis of modality was developed independently by Kripke, Jaakko Hintikka, Stig Kanger, and others. A recent investigation of model structures for interpreting tenses is van Benthem (1983). On the contextual interpretations of modality touched on at the end of the lecture, see especially Kratzer (1977).

LECTURE III

The paper referred to at the beginning of the lecture is Bach (1968). For those who would like some idea of what the first interactions between linguists and philosophers in the late 1960s were like, Davidson and Harman (1972) is a good source. The expository material on complex CNPs and NPs is again drawn from *PTQ* and references for Lecture I are still apposite. Russell's interpretations of singular definites such as *the present King of France* is set forth in his paper "On Denoting" (1905).

LECTURE IV

Barwise and Cooper (1981) was the paper which pointed many semanticists toward the generalized quantifier perspective on natural language interpretations in full generality, and it is probably still the best place to start for tracking this line of development. Since that time many studies on generalized quantifiers in natural language have been conducted (a recent publication with a number of papers, mostly pretty technical, is Gärdenfors, 1987). On *there*-sentences: Milsark (1974) is a standard reference mainly on the syntax but with important semantic observations. The account of polarity items is based primarily on Ladusaw (1979). Linebarger (1981) argues for an alternative, syntactic account. A recent important study is Zwarts (1986, in Dutch; an expanded English version is in preparation).

LECTURE V

Recently, a strong interest in categorial approaches to syntax and semantics has arisen; see, for example, Oehrle, Bach, and Wheeler (1987). Categorial grammar was initiated by Ajdukiewicz (1935) and continued by Lambek (1961) and Bar-Hillel (1953).

Among the workers who initiated model-theoretic approaches to the semantics of natural languages about the same time as Montague and have developed their work since that time should be mentioned: Keenan (Keenan and Faltz, 1985), Cresswell (1973), and Terence Parsons (early work that has never been published).

Discussion of problems of "sortal incorrectness" in Montague semantics may be found in Waldo (1979), who builds on Thomason (1972). Partee (1976) contain a number of papers illustrating early extensions to Montague's work. On kinds, see Carlson (1977); on plurals, Bennett (1974), Link (1983), Landman (1987); on propositional expressions in English, Delacruz (1976); on the semantics of nouns and classifiers in a language with no obligatory singular/plural distinction (Thai), Stein (1981). Parsons (1979) is an attempt to deal with the problem of syntactic inflation in standard Montague grammar in an interesting way by using schemata for the types corresponding to various syntactic categories.

LECTURE VI

Two recent books that devote primary attention to problems about belief and other propositional attitudes within possible worlds framework are Cresswell (1985) and Stalnaker (1984). For a start within the program of situation semantics (mentioned briefly in the next lecture), see Barwise and Perry (1983). On events, processes, states, Dowty (1979) gives a good survey of earlier work with references; see also Mourelatos (1978). Further references to the topics addressed herein are given in the endnote to Lecture VII. On properties, my basic source here is Chierchia (1984), who draws on work by Cocchiarella; see also Turner (1984) and watch for forthcoming joint work by Chierchia and Turner. On names as rigid designators, Kripke (1972).

LECTURE VII

In this lecture, I again draw upon G. Carlson (1977), Chierchia (1982, 1984), and Link (1983). Cresswell's theory is set forth in his (1973). Thematic relations were first extensively discussed in Gruber (1965). Fillmore's (1968) case theory is a partly independent but similar development. For an initial incorporation of such notions into the stream of "standard" transformational grammar, see Jackendoff (1972); van Riemsdijk and Williams (1986: Ch. 15) may serve as a convenient introduction to the place of θ-theory in more recent transformational frameworks. Some of the proposals mentioned in the first part of this lecture are discussed in Bach (1986a, 1986b). For a careful treatment of events and their manifestations as space-time locations, see Hinrichs (1985); space-time locations play a primary role in situation semantics as well. The few model-theoretic approaches to problems of thematic relations are: Chierchia (1984), Carlson (1984), Dowty (forthcoming). Davidson's important papers on events, actions, and related problems are conveniently reprinted (with some additional commentary) in Davidson (1980). Terry Parsons has written a series of papers (1980, 1985, forthcoming) in which Montague-style fragments are proposed or presented for an analysis of English that makes explicit syntactic use of thematic roles in a Davidsonian vein. For situation semantics see Barwise and Perry (1983) and the literature cited there; a number of critiques of the theory appear in *Linguistics and Philosophy* 8.1 (February 1985). Heim (1982) and Kamp (1981) are the basic references for their theories. Pelletier (1979) is a useful collection of papers on the philosophical problems of mass terms.

LECTURE VIII

On the problem of "psychological reality" in semantics, see Partee (1979).

Putnam's papers on the philosophy of language are conveniently available in Putnam (1975). The "later" Wittgenstein's thoughts on language and "language-games" may be found in (1958). Jerry Fodor has recently published a book called *Psychosemantics* (1987). On "mental models": Johnson-Laird (1983). Gil (1982) is an important study of the variation (across languages) and problems of interpreting quantifiers. On the question of the interpretation of NPs, see Williams (1983) and Partee (1987).

Current research in semantics of the sort I have concentrated on here is being conducted throughout the world now. Much of the research, as in other active fields, is reported on in "semi-publications" that range from photocopies and computer mail to more or less regular publications of "working papers" by various research groups. Papers on semantics now appear fairly regularly in most of the journals that include work on theoretical linguistics. Some of the more important journals that are more centrally focussed on semantics and the philosophy of language from a linguistic point of view are: *Linguistics and Philosophy, Journal of Semantics, Journal of Philosophical Logic*. Regular conferences take place around the world that are devoted primarily to semantic issues (for example, at universities located in Amsterdam and Konstanz).

REFERENCES

Ajdukiewicz, Kazimierz. 1935. Die syntaktische Konnexität. *Studia Philosophica* 1: 1–27. English translation in Storrs McCall, ed., *Polish Logic: 1920–1939* (Oxford University Press, 1976).

Arnauld Antoine. 1964. *The Art of Thinking.* James Dickoff and Patricia James, trans. (First published in 1662.) Indianapolis, New York, Kansas City: Bobbs-Merrill.

Bach, Emmon. 1968. Nouns and noun phrases. In Emmon Bach and Robert T. Harms, eds., *Universals in Linguistic Theory* (New York: Holt, Rinehart and Winston), pp. 90–122. Reprinted in Davidson and Harman, 1975.

————. 1986a. The algebra of events. *Linguistics and Philosophy* 9: 5–16.

————. 1986b. Natural language metaphysics. In R. Barcan Marcus, G. J. W. Dorn, P. Weingartner, eds., *Logic, Methodology and Philosophy of Science VII* (Amsterdam *et al.*: North-Holland), pp. 573–595.

Bar-Hillel, Yehoshua. 1953. A quasi-arithmetical notation of syntactic description. *Language* 29: 47–58.

Barwise, Jon and Robin Cooper. 1981. Generalized Quantifiers and Natural Language. *Linguistics and Philosophy* 4: 159–219.

———and John Perry. 1983. *Situations and Attitudes.* Cambridge, Massachusetts: MIT Press (Bradford Books).

Bennett, Michael. 1974. Some extensions of a Montague fragment of English. Ph.D. dissertation: University of California, Los Angeles.

van Benhem, J. F. A. K. 1983. *The Logic of Time.* Dordrecht: Reidel.

———. 1986. *Essays in Logical Semantics.* Dordrecht: Reidel.

Bresnan, Joan, ed. 1982. *The Mental Representation of Grammatical Relations.* Cambridge, Massachusetts: MIT Press.

Carlson, Greg N. 1977. Reference to kinds in English. Ph.D. dissertation: University of Massachusetts, Amherst.

———. 1984. Thematic roles and their role in semantic interpretation. *Linguistics* 22: 259–279.

Chierchia, Gennaro. 1982. Bare plurals, mass nouns, and nominalization. *Proceedings of the First West Coast Conference on Formal Linguistics:* pp. 243–255.

———. 1984. Topics in the Syntax and Semantics of Infinitives and Gerunds. Ph.D. dissertation: University of Massachusetts, Amherst.

Chomsky, Noam. 1957. *Syntactic Structures.* The Hague: Mouton.

———. 1981/82. *Lectures on Government and Binding.* Dordrecht: Foris.

Cresswell, Max J. 1973. *Logics and Languages.* London: Methuen.

———. 1985. *Structured Meanings.* Cambridge, Massachusetts: MIT Press (Bradford Books).

Davidson, Donald. 1980. *Essays on Actions and Events.* Oxford: Clarendon Press.

———and Gilbert Harman, eds. 1972. *Semantics of Natural Language.* Dordrecht: Reidel.

———and Gilbert Harman, eds. 1975. *The Logic of Grammar.* Encino and Belmont, California: Dickenson.

Davis, Steven and Marianne Mithun, eds. 1979. *Linguistics, Philosophy, and Montague Grammar.* Austin and London: The University of Texas Press.

Delacruz, Enrique B. 1976. Factives and proposition level construction in Montague Grammar. In Partee, 1976, pp. 177–199.

Dowty, David R., Robert E. Wall, and Stanley Peters. 1981. *Introduction to Montague Semantics*. Dordrecht: Reidel.

Dowty, David R. 1979. *Word Meaning and Montague Grammar*. Dordrecht: Reidel.

————. (forthcoming) On the semantic content of the notion of "thematic role." To appear in G. Chierchia, B. H. Partee, and R. Turner, eds., *Properties, Types, and Meaning*.

Fillmore, Charles J. 1968. The case for case. In Emmon Bach and Robert T. Harms, eds. *Universals in Linguistic Theory* (New York: Holt, Rinehart and Winston), pp. 1–88.

Fodor, Janet Dean. 1977. *Semantics: Theories of Meaning in Generative Grammar*. New York: Crowell.

Fodor, Jerry A. 1987. *Psychosemantics: The Problem of meaning in the Philosophy of Mind*. Cambridge, Massachusetts: MIT Press (Bradford Books).

Gamut, L. T. F. [pseud.] 1982. *Logica, taal en betekinis: Intensionale logica en logische grammatica*. Vols. 1, 2. Utrecht/Antwerpen: Het Spectrum.

Gärdenfors, Peter, ed. 1987. *Generalized Quantifiers*. Dordrecht: Reidel.

Geach, P. T. 1962. *Reference and Generality*. Ithaca, New York: Cornell University Press.

————. 1972. A program for syntax. In Davidson and Harman (1972), pp. 483–497.

Gil, David. 1982. Quantifier scope, linguistic variation, and natural language semantics. *Linguistics and Philosophy* 5: 421–472.

Grice. H. P. 1975. Logic and conversation. In Davidson and Harman (1975), pp. 64–75.

Gruber, Jeffrey. 1965. Studies in Lexical Relations. Ph.D. dissertation: Massachusetts Institute of Technology, Cambridge.

Heim, Irene R. 1982. The Semantics of Definite and Indefinite Noun Phrases. Ph.D. dissertation: University of Massachusetts, Amherst.

Hinrichs, Erhard. 1985. A compositional semantics for Aktionsarten and NP reference in English. Ph.D. dissertation: The Ohio State University.

Jackendoff, Ray S. 1972. *Semantic Interpretation in Generative Grammar*. Cambridge, Massachusetts: MIT Press.

————. 1983. *Semantics and Cognition*. Cambridge, Massachusetts: MIT Press.

Janssen, Theo. 1984. Individual concepts are useful. In Landman and Veltman (1984).

Johnson-Laird, Philip N. 1983. *Mental Models*. Cambridge, Massachusetts: Harvard University Press.

Kamp, J. A. W. 1975. Two theories about adjectives. In Keenan (1975), pp. 123–155.

Kamp, Hans. 1981. A theory of truth and semantic representation. In J. A. G. Groenendijk, T. M. V. Janssen, and M. B. J. Stokhof, eds., *Formal Methods in the Study of Language* (Amsterdam: Mathematisch Centrum) 1: 277–322.

Keenan, Edward L., ed. 1975. *Formal Semantics of Natural Language*. Cambridge: Cambridge University Press.

————and Leonard M. Faltz. 1985. *Boolean Semantics for Natural Language*. Dordrecht: Reidel.

Klima, Edward S. 1964. Negation in English. In Jerry A. Foder and Jerrold J. Katz, eds., *The Structure of Language* (Englewood Cliffs, New Jersey: Prentice-Hall), pp. 246–323.

Kratzer, Angelika. 1977. What 'must' and 'can' must and can mean. *Linguistics and Philosophy* 1: 337–355.

————. 1978. *Semantik der Rede: Kontexttheorie = Modalwörter = Konditionalisätze*. Königstein/Ts.: Scriptor.

————. Forthcoming. An investigation of the lumps of thought. (University of Massachusetts, Amherst.)

Kripke, Saul A. 1972. Naming and necessity. In Davidson and Harman, 1972: pp. 253–355.

————. 1963. Semantical considerations on modal logic. *Acta Philosophica Fennica* 16: 83–94. Reprinted in Linsky, 1971.

Ladusaw, William. 1979. Polarity sensitivity as Inherent Scope Relations. Ph.D. dissertation: The University of Texas, Austin.

Lambek, Joachim. 1961. On the calculus of syntactic types. In R. Jakobson, ed., *Structure of Language and its Mathematical Aspects*. Providence, Rhode Island: Proceedings of Symposia in Applied Mathematics, XII, American Mathematical Society, pp. 166–178.

Landman, Fred. 1986. *Toward a theory of Information: The Status of Partial*

Objects in Semantics. Proefschrift: Universiteit van Amsterdam. (= GRASS 6, Dordrecht: Foris).

————. [1987] Groups. Unpublished ms. (University of Massachusetts, Amherst; a shorter version of this paper was presented at the 1987 Amsterdam Colloquium and will appear in the Proceedings).

Lewis, David. 1968. Counterpart theory and quantified modal logic. *Journal of Philosophy* 65: 113–126. Reprinted in Lewis, 1983.

————. 1972. General semantics. In Davidson and Harman, 1972: pp. 169–218.

————. 1983, 1986. *Philosophical Papers.* Volume I [1983], Volume II [1986]. New York and Oxford: Oxford University Press.

Linebarger, M. C. 1980. The Grammar of Negative Polarity. Ph.D. dissertation: Massachusetts Institute of Technology, Cambridge.

Link, Godehard. 1979. *Montague-Grammatik.* München: Wilhelm Fink.

————. 1983. The logical analysis of plurals and mass terms. In R. Bäuerle, Ch. Schwarze, and A. von Stechow, eds., *Meaning, Use, and Interpretation of Language* (Berlin: de Gruyter), pp. 302–323.

Linsky, Leonard, ed. 1971. *Reference and Modality.* London: Oxford University Press.

Milsark, Gary. 1974. Existential Sentences in English. Ph.D. dissertation: Massachusetts Institute of Technology, Cambridge.

Montague, Richard. 1974. *Formal Philosophy.* Richmond H. Thomason, ed. New Haven, Connecticut: Yale University Press.

Mourelatos, Alexander. 1978. Events, processes, and states. *Linguistics and Philosophy* 2: 415–434.

Oehrle, Richard, Emmon Bach, and Deirdre Wheeler, eds. 1987. *Categorial Grammar and Natural Language Structure.* Dordrecht: Reidel.

Parsons, Terence. 1979. Type theory and ordinary language. In David and Mithun, 1979, pp. 127–151.

————. 1980. Modifiers and quantifiers in natural language. *Canadian Journal of Philosophy,* supplementary vol. 6: 29–60.

————. 1985. Underlying events in the logical analysis of English. In Ernest LePore and Brian P. McLaughlin, eds., *Actions and Events: Perspectives on the Philosophy of Donald Davidson* (London: Blackwell), pp. 235–267.

———. Forthcoming. The progressive in English: events, states and processes. (Ms.: University of California, Irvine.)

Partee, Barbara H., ed. 1976. *Montague Grammar*. New York, et al.: Academic Press.

———. 1987. Noun phrase interpretation and type-shifting principles. In J. Groenendijk, D. de Jongh, and M. Stokhof, eds., *Studies in Discourse Representation Theory and the Theory of Generalized Quantifiers*. (= GRASS 8: Dordrecht: Foris), pp. 115–143.

Pelletier, Francis Jeffry, ed. 1979. *Mass Terms: Some Philosophical Problems*. Dordrecht: Reidel.

Putnam, Hilary. 1975. *Mind, Language and Reality, Philosophical Papers: Volume 2*. Cambridge: Cambridge University Press.

van Riemsdijk, Henk and Edwin Williams. 1986. *Introduction to the Theory of Grammar*. Cambridge, Massachusetts: MIT Press.

Russell, Bertrand. 1905. On denoting. *Mind* 14: 479–493. Reprinted in Davidson and Harman, 1975.

Stalnaker, Robert C. 1984. *Inquiry*. Cambridge, Massachusetts: MIT Press (Bradford Books).

Stein, Mark J. 1981. Quantification in Thai. Ph.D. dissertation, University of Massachusetts, Amherst.

Strawson, P. F. 1950. On referring. In P. F. Strawson, *Logico-Linguistic Papers* (London: Methuen; 1971), pp. 1–27. (First published in *Mind* 59 (N.S.), 1950.)

Thomason, Richmond. 1972. A semantic theory of sortal incorrectness. *Journal of Philosophical Logic* 1: 209–258.

Turner, Raymond. 1983. Montague semantics, nominalization and Scott's domains. *Linguistics and Philosophy* 6: 259–288.

Veltman, Frank. 1985. Logics for conditionals. Proefschrift: Universiteit van Amsterdam.

Waldo, James. 1979. A PTQ semantics for sortal incorrectness. In Davis and Mithun, 1979, pp. 311–331.

Williams, Edwin. 1983. Semantic vs. syntactic categories. *Linguistics and Philosophy* 6: 423–446.

Wittgenstein, Ludwig. 1958. *Philosophical Investigations*. Third edition. Translated by G. E. M. Anscombe. (Includes German text.) New York: Macmillan.

Zwarts, Frans. 1986. Categoriale grammatica en algebraïsche semantiek. Proefschrift: Rijksuniversiteit te Groningen.

INDEX

Differences :

① lecture format
② use of formalism
③ very little explanation of what a linguist is (eg. 2)